A GARDEN FOR YOU

A practical guide to tools, equipment and design for older
people and people with disabilities

Fred Walden

Disabled Living Foundation
London

First published 1997
ISBN 0-901908-69-X

British Library Cataloguing in Publication Data
A catalogue record of this book is available from the British Library.

All information is provided without legal responsibility. It is advisable to
check all product details with the supplier before ordering.

Contents

Acknowledgements

The Disabled Living Foundation would like to thank the following people and organisations for their advice and help in the production of this book:

Fred Walden, who compiled this book;

the staff, clients and volunteers from the Mary Marlborough Centre, Headington, Oxford;

the staff at West & Sons Garden Centre, Headington, Oxford;

all the manufacturers who supplied equipment or technical advice, particularly Wolf-Tools, Erin-Gardena, Peta (UK) and Black & Decker for their prompt and encouraging response;

Jane Peart, the illustrator, for her clear and accurate line drawings.

Foreword

by Professor Stefan Buczacki

 There are, I'm told, some twenty-two million gardens in this country; and thus, I assume, at least twenty-two million gardeners. A love of gardens and gardening is embedded deep in our national psyche. It is a pursuit that provides at the same time satisfaction, recreation and escapism.

But, as those of us fortunate enough to be able-bodied, dig our trenches, erect our runner bean poles and prune our apple trees, how often do we give thought to those less fortunate: those, once fit, active and as enthusiastic as we are about gardening who have, through illness or accident, found even the simplest of tasks to be a major undertaking; or those born with a disability for whom every gardening operation has always been difficult?

Not so many years ago, I think the answer was 'hardly ever'. More recently, the importance of catering for older people and people with disabilities in their gardening activities has become much more widely recognised: not least because the very activity itseslf has come to be seen as so beneficial and therapeutic.

This book has given me much pleasure and satisfaction in the way that I can see it will both help and inspire less able gardeners to gain as much from their hobby as I do. I am deeply impressed by the sheer commonsense of it all and by the way that even the aspects that I, in my naivety, would have thought easy, do in reality need careful planning.

There is no better example of this than the subject of weight. While it's pretty evident to any gardener that a light tool will be less arduous to use than a heavy one, it's not so immediately obvious that this is compounded and magnified out of all proportion if your limbs are weak. To have the weights as well as the dimensions of tools listed routinely will be a boon therefore.

I commend this book very warmly, both to older people and people with disabilities themselves and to those involved in their care and rehabilitation. If it enables just one more individual to share my love of this wonderful activity, it will have succeeded admirably. I suspect, however, that in reality, it will help thousands.

Introduction

Many thousands of books have been written on the subject of gardening and probably more than a hundred for people with special needs. Initially, most of the latter were written by people with some medical training who were the first to 'discover' the therapeutic benefits of gardening.

This book aims to provide straightforward, unbiased information primarily for people who have an interest in gardening but who, because they are older or have a condition that restricts them in some way, may find well designed equipment or special techniques helpful to them.

People with more complicated or serious conditions must take particular care, and support is available from a number of sources (see Appendix 2).

The first chapter on design provides only a brief introduction to this subject since it is covered comprehensively in other books to which the reader is referred (see Appendix 3, Further reading). For the same reason, little advice on plants is included.

This book's particular emphasis is on tools and equipment (Chapter 2) and on techniques for particular disabilities (Chapter 3).

The tools and equipment mentioned have been thoroughly tested by the compiler and by the clients, engineers and therapists at the Mary Marlborough Centre in Oxford. The companies supplying them are, to the best of the author's knowledge, reliable; they also understand the needs of older people and people with disabilities and are willing to discuss any problems and provide spares.

Only a few of the hundreds of items available are covered in this book, but the compiler has tried to select the best and the most relevant.

Chapter 3 - on tools and techniques for people with specific disabilities - can be used as a short cut and a checklist for therapists. However, since the division into specific disabilities is necessarily somewhat arbitrary, some people may find that they have to consult more than one section to find the answers they need.

Happy gardening!

DLF GUIDES FOR OLDER PEOPLE AND PEOPLE WITH DISABILITIES

FLYING HIGH a practical guide to a travel. 32 pages - £2.50 inc p&p

ALL DRESSED UP a guide to choosing clothes and useful dressing techniques. 124 pages - £4.95 inc p&p

A KITCHEN FOR YOU a practic guide to equipment and design. 172 pages - £6.95 inc p&p

These guides are available from the DLF,
380-384 Harrow Road, London W9 2HU
Tel 0171 289 6111. Fax 0171 266 2922

1 Garden design

Since this book is intended for people with many different needs, the subject of garden design cannot be covered in any great detail. However, some basic considerations apply to almost everyone with mobility impairments.

'Access' is the key word and, if your physical condition restricts your mobility, you will require better access than someone who is fully mobile.

Paths are the most crucial element in garden design and merit considerable thought. Common problems are steps and uneven and unstable surfacing. As you plan the paths in your garden you will need to consider the layout of the soil and lawn areas.

Steps can be avoided with ramps or improved by making them shallower, wider and deeper. You may also need to install handrails.

Smaller, narrower growing areas provide better horizontal access but, for many people, the soil may need to be raised to a more convenient level. Do not rush into building raised structures until you have tried to use them and also considered tools that may help you to overcome any problems (see Chapter 2); the amount of work involved and the expense can be off-putting and can create other problems.

If your garden is small, your mobility restricted or your time is limited, then patio and container gardening may be the solution.

Maintenance is another aspect that ought to be considered when you are designing your garden. With modern equipment and carefully chosen plants it is possible to create an attractive garden that can be maintained with very little work.

It may be less interesting to look at and expensive to build, but it will provide a garden that is worry free and involve you in little ongoing expense.

Some people enjoy designing a garden; others enjoy maintaining it; while others like to sit back and watch it grow. Whatever your preference, do not be afraid to make changes; virtually all plants and structures can be replaced or rebuilt and you can always learn from your mistakes!

If possible, carry out any changes in late autumn and early spring - plants are more easily moved at those times and there are fewer other garden tasks to deal with. Also, contractors, if needed, are likely to be less busy than during the hectic summer months.

BASIC PRINCIPLES

When considering garden design, bear the following basic principles in mind:

- be realistic about how much gardening you want to do and how much you are likely to do;
- make some sketches or, even better, drawings to scale;
- think ahead about how large the plants will grow;
- provide some paved areas near the house and do not forget shade and shelter;
- use the natural conditions of your garden to their best advantage rather than trying to fight them. For example, grow marsh and bog plants in damp areas, alpines in stony soil and Mediterranean plants in hot dry areas.

DESIGN AND CONSTRUCTION

If you decide to commission someone to design your garden for you, bear in mind that you will have to pay a separate fee for the design. The construction can then either be organised and supervised by the designer for an additional fee or be undertaken by someone else.

You will probably need some form of help with the construction. Whether you are doing it yourself or seeking help, it is worth consulting a book on garden design. *Landscape design for the elderly and disabled* and the *RHS's Garden structures* are recommended (see Appendix 3, Further reading). These books will probably be available at your local library.

PATHS, STEPS, HANDRAILS AND RAMPS

Paths

The most crucial element of garden design for older people and people with disabilities is the provision of good access to the garden by safe, easy-to-use paths. The downside of this, especially for wheelchair users, is that growing areas will be sacrificed to surfacing and that you will also be incurring additional expense.

An accessible garden, consisting of a number of small but interconnected areas, can, if properly constructed, look very attractive and is extremely practical. The old fashioned parterre garden is an example of this.

By having more paths and smaller soil areas it it easier to use the 'no dig' or 'low-dig' technique. Because the soil can be worked from the path and is not trodden on, it does not become so compacted and needs less digging. If a good quantity of organic material is included at the start then it may be possible to garden for up to 10 years with little more than light hoeing and shallow cultivation. Mulching may be required to preserve moisture and add nutrients. This technique has been tried extensively at Ryton Organic Gardens with good results.

Paths can be constructed from many suitable materials, and using a variety of these can be a feature in itself. The decision as to how wide you make a path will depend on who will be using it.

Narrower paths can be made with turning spaces for wheelchairs at intervals, although it will be easier to work from a wide path with more space in which to manoeuvre.

A parterre garden

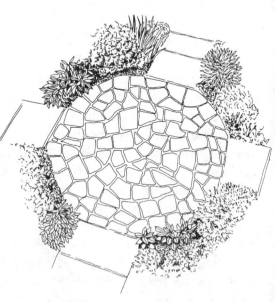

Four paths leading to a turning point

Edging the path

Most edging on paths is used to stabilise the material (ie gravel) or to keep back soil. However, a small raised edge to the path could have other benefits for some disabled people. Visually impaired people can often use edging as a tapping rail or for contrast to find their way; it can also be used to prevent wheelchair users from running off the edge and into soft soil.

But edging can also be a hazard and cause people to trip or fall. When considering edging, the main factor to be taken into account should be the mobility skills of the people using the path. A very low edge may be enough to let wheelchair users know that they have hit something but not high enough to tip up the chair.

Materials for paths and other surfacing

Brick paviors

Traditionally 80mm thick and designed to carry vehicles, brick paviors are now available in thinner (40mm) versions for the garden. Not only cheaper but easier to handle, these can be bought in many different colours and some have interlocking nodes. If laid properly on the right foundation, they form a very stable and attractive path that can be altered or recycled at a later date.

The advantages of paviors are that they are attractive, strong, slip-

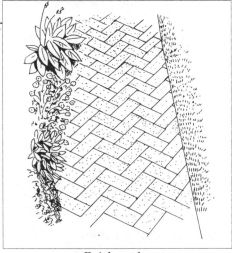

Brick path

resistant, non-reflective, recyclable and frostproof.

The disadvantages are the expense and the time and skill needed to lay them down properly.

Old housebricks

It is possible to make an attractive, cheap path using old housebricks. However, some have very smooth and potentially slippery surfaces while others may be subject to frost damage and eventually erode so that their surface becomes uneven.

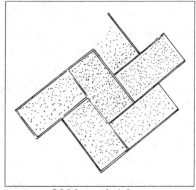

Old housebricks

Concrete

Cheaper than paviors but not as attractive, concrete is a flexible material which can be coloured, painted and given a slip-resistant texture. One drawback is that, once laid, it is not easily altered or removed. In addition, badly built paths crack and decay and can cost a lot to remove.

Concrete paths do not need a raised edge to make them stable.

Gravel

A gravel path is often the cheapest solution but can be a major problem for wheelchair users. Keeping weeds at bay is another problem that should be considered, although you must balance this against the aesthetic appeal of the more natural look of a gravel path.

The best results will be achieved if you use material with a maximum diameter of 5mm over graded layers of courser material and then compact it with a plate

vibrator (which can be hired from most hire centres).
Some form of edge may be required to stabilise the path
and prevent weeds from encroaching.

Tarmac

Like concrete, this material is flexible, can be coloured
and provides a strong, smooth but slip-resistant surface.
To give the path a more natural look, small gravel
chippings can be rolled into the surface. The drawbacks
are that specialist labour is required to lay tarmac and
that wheelchair tyres may sink into the path if the tarmac
is exposed to strong sunlight on long summer days.

Concrete slabs

Concrete slabs are probably the most popular form of
hard surfacing in the garden and, when correctly laid,
form an ideal surface for all users. An important factor to
bear in mind is the texture of the slabs, as some have a
smooth, reflective and slippery surface while others are
extremely rough and uneven. Fortunately, most slabs fall
between the two extremes and are available in a wide
range of colours and sizes. Choose the texture to suit
your needs. For large areas, consider using slabs of
different sizes to avoid monotony.

The disadvantages of concrete slabs are that they are
expensive, that skill and strength are needed to lay them
and that weeds are likely to grow in the cracks betweeen
the slabs.

Wood decking

Widely used in the United States and becoming more
popular in the UK, wood decking looks attractive but
can become slippery when wet and deteriorate quickly.

It is essential to use pressure treated timber. Chicken wire can be stapled onto slopes to provide grip - this looks unsightly at first, but will 'weather' in time.

Grass

Grass, the most natural of surfaces, is rarely practical since it is constantly changing shape and holds water like a sponge. However, if it is well mown and rolled, wheelchairs users should be able to manoeuvre on it easily in the dry summer months.

    The advantages of grass are that it is soft to fall on, is aesthetically pleasing and is easy to grow.

Portapath

For temporary access, this green plastic material can be rolled out over lawns or soil. The interconnecting panels (see p 62) can form a narrow path for walking or, if three widths are laid side be side, for wheelchairs. It is fairly expensive and weeds will grow in the gaps but it is easy to lay (and remove).

Portapath

Steps and handrails

If steps are a necessity, make sure that they are wide, shallow and deep, that the texture is slip-resistant, and that there is no overhang which might catch your feet. Also, be careful to keep foliage from encroaching on the steps and do not plant overhanging trees that drop fruit or leaves if you can help it. If this is problem, replace such trees with an evergreen plant.

For ambulant disabled people or those who are slightly unsteady on their feet, handrails, especially on steps, may be required. The height and length of the rail will vary depending on the individual but all must be structurally sound. If the rail is fixed against a wall, you will have to buy a metal or wooden rail with fittings. If the handrails are free standing, strong and natural looking rails can be made from lengths of tree branches.

Shallow steps and rustic wooden handrails

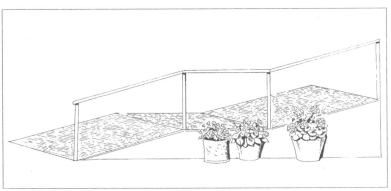

Wheelchair ramp

Ramps

Ramps are essential for wheelchair users who need to access different levels. To minimise expense, consider using the slope of your garden to maximum benefit by

CREATING A RAISED AREA IN A SLOPING GARDEN

Cut away parts to
make terraces

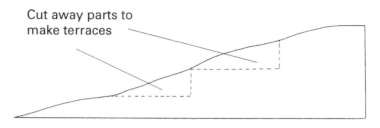

Sloping garden (before)

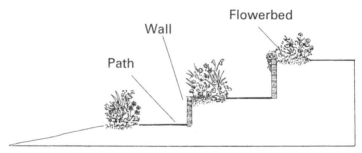

Flowerbed

Wall

Path

Sloping garden (after) with ramp and terracing

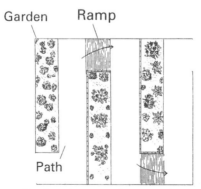

Garden   Ramp

Path

Plan of raised area after work completed

creating terraces. This can be a way of making raised growing areas and solving your access problems.

By placing paths and ramps parallel to the edge of the terrace and creating narrow borders along this edge, wheelchair users will be able to cultivate the terraces. Remember, however, that working from a wheelchair is only possible on a very shallow slope.

Ramps can be constructed from all the materials used for paths but the best is usually concrete.

All ramps should have a gradient of at least 1:15, although 1:20 is preferable. Long ramps over 3m should have a flat resting area and possibly a passing place.

The main problem when making ramps is that people often underestimate the length required to overcome the height.

Ramps can look very unsightly and this is one reason why public gardens are reluctant to build them. However, if carefully designed, ramps can be unobtrusive and even become an attractive feature.

RAISED GROWING AREAS

Raised growing areas include raised beds, containers and other structures. Cutting into the natural slope of the garden and using a retaining wall to hold back the soil is the easiest way to create such an area.

Piling up soil against a garden wall and building a retaining wall is almost as easy.

The most expensive, awkward and unnatural-looking method is to build a free-standing structure. However, the advantage of such a structure is that access to it can be gained from all sides.

Free-standing structures

In order to provide the best access, the shape of the structure should be long, narrow and rectangular. Curves are also possible but are difficult to build.

In addition to the expense involved in building them, the other disadvantages of free-standing structures are that working sideways on from a wheelchair will soon become uncomfortable and anyone who is standing will need toeholes so that he or she can get close to the plants.

The height and width of the structure will depend on what it is to be used for; in an institutional setting, for example, it is best to provide a variety of heights. As a guide only, the width should be no more than 600mm for independent use (or 1200mm if there is access from both sides).

Heights are best determined by experimenting with a mock-up designed for the individual or individuals concerned. For example, two wheelchair users of the same height may prefer different dimensions depending on their particular disabilities. Working with your shoulders flat and the soil below elbow level are the best guidelines you can follow. The tools that you intend using and the plants to be grown should also be taken into consideration.

Points to consider

- The higher the structure, the more substantial the building material will have to be. However, the walls should, preferably, be as thin as possible so that the user can get close to the soil.
- Materials like natural stone tend to be fairly thick, while timber panelling is much thinner.

MAKING A RAISED BED IN A PATIO OR YARD

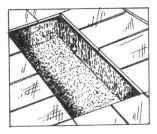

Take up 1 or 2 rows of
slabs, then dig a hole
to about a third of the
height of the slabs

Into the hole insert
the slab upright into
the corner

Infill with rubble
behind the slab to fix
it in position

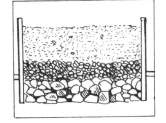

When all the slabs
have been inserted,
add a layer of course
grit and top-up with
an open structured
compost

- Whatever materials you use, line the inside with polythene to stop the soil being washed out and to reduce dampness and corrosion.
- The sides of a high structure may have to be tied together to prevent them bowing out.
- Consider putting a standpipe on, or near, the structure as drying out is often a problem.
- Provide weep holes at the bottom for drainage.

Raised bed using paving stones

Materials for free-standing structures

The material you use will depend on your budget, your needs and your aesthetic preferences. It is advisable to consult a builder, landscape architect and/or specialist book (see Appendix 3, Stoneham T and Thoday P).

In this publication, the various features you should consider are outlined. The more elaborate structures will probably be beyond the ability of the average disabled DIY person unless he or she has the help of a strong labourer.

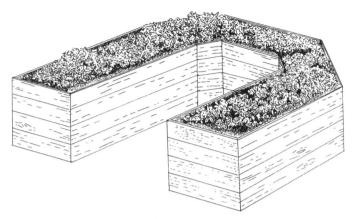

Raised bed made of wood panels and posts

At this point it is worth considering how long you want the structure to last. Wood is probably the easiest material to use and, if pressure treated with chemicals, could last 20 years.

- Concrete slabs are ugly and have no toe holes, but they are cheap and have thin edges so that the user has good access to the soil. The structure is relatively easy to construct (see diagrams).

Raised bed made of logroll

HOW TO MAKE A CONTAINER OF SANDBAGS MADE FROM OLD TIGHTS

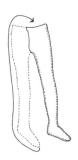  

1 Take an old pair of tights and put one leg inside the other

2. Pour dry soil into the foot of the tights

3 Firmly knot the tights

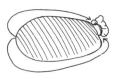 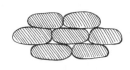 

4 Fold empty half back on itself and knot again

5 Now build a container

6 The finished container when planted

- Brick is versatile, attractive and not too thick, but it is expensive, requires skilled labour to install and will be damaged by frost unless engineering brick or coping stones are used on the top. Also, sulphur-resistant cement may be needed to combat water corrosion.
- Natural stone is attractive and versatile but it can be expensive and is likely to be thick so that easy access to the soil is more difficult.
- Wood panels and wood posts are attractive, fairly inexpensive, and not too thick, but they will rot unless pressure treated. Also, beware of splinters! These can be constructed on a DIY basis, or purpose-built, flexible modules (Designwood) are available from MCI Timply.
- Logroll is attractive, easy to install and reasonably priced. However, it is only practical for structures up to about 300mm high.
- Sandbags, made from old tights, garden soil and sand are cheap, can look attractive when weathered and are durable, but are time consuming to make.

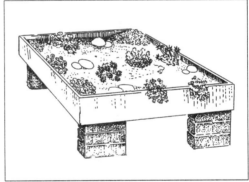

Shallow wooden container on bricks suitable for alpines

CONTAINERS AND PATIO GARDENING

If, because of your disability, your activities are very restricted, or you do not want the worry of a

Baths and stone sinks can be used as containers

conventional garden with a lawn and open areas of soil, then a patio garden may be the answer.

This type of gardening is growing in popularity among people who lead busy lives and want to garden when it suits them. The only disadvantage of a patio garden is that watering is more crucial if you have small containers or thirsty plants. By carefully choosing both containers and plants and using silicon crystals, even watering can be negligable except during summer heatwaves.

Ideally, your patio garden should contain an outside water tap so that watering is a simple task using a hosepipe or automatic system. Another good idea is to collect rainwater from a drainpipe as a backup.

Watering requirements will depend on a number of factors, one being the aspect of the garden and how exposed it is. The more hard surfacing there is, the more heat will be retained and the hotter the garden will become. Some shade is important for the personal comfort of the person working, or sitting, in the garden, and this will also enable a greater variety of plants to survive.

Containers

People gardening from a wheelchair or those who cannot bend will find that half barrels make ideal plant containers as the plants in them can be reached easily. However, any tub-like container can be used depending on the style you prefer. Chimney pots also make good plant containers, while old tyres are not quite so attractive!

Stone sinks can be mounted on bricks or slabs and covered with a mixture of peat and cement so that they blend into their surroundings.

The depth of any container is crucial. Some have been purpose built for wheelchair gardeners but, in order to provide leg space, their depth has to be compromised. This leaves them unsuitable for anything but alpines.

Different ideas for container using a toilet (left) and three sections of a sewer pipe (right)

Among other items that have been used successfully as containers are baths, toilets (bowls and cisterns), old watertanks and large concrete sewer pipes.

Numerous containers in which strawberries and even potatoes can be grown are available, and some containers (with a reservoir) are self-watering.

Tips on using containers

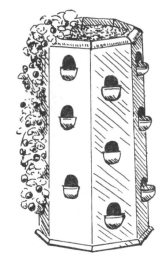

Growing strawberries in a special container

- To help the container to retain moisture better, use silicon crystals.
- Make sure that there is a waterbutt or hosepipe nearby.
- Consider buying or borrowing sack wheels if you have to move tubs.
- Use an open structured, free draining compost and mix in a slow release granular fertiliser.
- Use a wooden platform with castors if the tubs have to be moved frequently.

Hanging baskets

A well planted hanging basket can look very attractive but will require constant watering and will also be quite heavy to

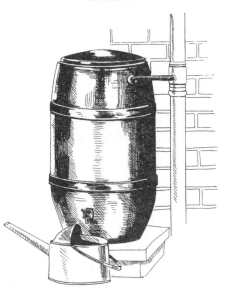

Make sure there is a water butt nearby

move. For people with reduced strength or mobility they are rather impractical and can cause strain and injuries.

Two items of equipment that can make life easier for those with sufficient strength are a pulley system or the Hi-lo device (available from most garden centres and DIY shops) for raising and lowering and an extending lance for daily (or twice daily) watering.

As with any container, the addition of water-storing silicon crystals (the granules start off as crystals and then expand into a gel to hold up to 400 times their own weight in water) will cut down the amount of watering.

OTHER KINDS OF GARDENING

Start a garden club in your area

If you are so severely restricted by your disability or personal situation that conventional forms of gardening are impossible, you can, nevertheless, continue to maintain your interest and hobby in a number of other ways.

Small scale gardening activities such as growing Bonzai trees can be as challenging and fascinating as any other kinds of gardening. Some of the more elaborate displays are in fact gardens or landscapes in miniature.

Designing a garden by computer

This kind of activity can be undertaken at a bench (inside or out) or even on a tray attached to a wheelchair.

As with any other type of gardening for disabled people the design of your facilities (whether your tools are stored on open shelving rather than in a cupboard, for example) will determine how much you can do and how independent you can be.

Collecting seeds and growing rare plants is another way that you can maintain your interest in gardening, or you could use your knowledge and organising skills to start a garden club in your area.

Growing houseplants, air plants and carniverous plants or creating a bottle garden, which does not involve using a great deal of strength and can be done in a fairly confined space, can be very satisfying and challenging activities.

Do not forget that the person who plans and supervises the garden has a very important part to play. With computers and design software, even the most severely disabled people can use their specialist knowledge and creativity to become the next Capability Brown or Gertrude Jekyl!

If you do not wish, or are unable, to take part in any of these activities, you can still sit in the garden and enjoy the sights and sounds while reading a book or chatting to friends - gardens are not just for working in!

2 Tools and equipment

As gardeners we seek to manage and control nature to create our own environment; if we leave the garden alone for any length of time we see what a dynamic force we are dealing with.

Any keen gardener maintaining a multitude of plants in a man-made landscape will need a number of tools. For older gardeners or gardeners with a disability, choosing which tools to use is particularly important.

One or two tools described in this chapter and in chapter 3 may suffice for most gardeners; for more advanced gardeners there is a tool for every task. The choice will depend on the style of your garden, your budget and whether you prefer to use technology or not.

Some people feel that using automatic watering systems and power tools is cheating; others will use every trick and shortcut to enable them to continue to manage the largest and most varied area possible.

It is estimated that each year British gardeners spend £2.6 billion on their hobby. It is not surprising, therefore, that so many new tools and gadgets appear on the market every year, many of them aimed at those who are getting older - the 'grey market'. One of the advantages of this is that most of the tools are so well designed that they benefit all gardeners; they can even prevent injuries and conditions from developing.

Many of the tools designed specifically for disabled people have not been a success. This is because these users fall into such diverse groups with a great variety of different, and often conflicting, needs.

However, many tools from standard ranges, if carefully chosen or adapted, can be perfectly suitable.

Buying equipment

The largest chains of DIY stores usually offer the best prices and stock a large range of equipment. However, if you are looking for more specialist equipment and advice, you should go to the nearest good garden centre.

Ideally, older gardeners and gardeners with disibiliities need to try out the equipment before buying, but this is normally impossible since the tool, once used, cannot be sold to someone else. However, one or two of the specialist gardening mail-order companies recognise this problem and offer a money-back guarantee. Mail order is not only convenient for some tools, it is the only option.

Some catalogues containing general equipment for disability may also include a page or two of gardening tools. Buying tools from these catalogues is usually the most expensive option. All companies should offer a money back option (excluding postage and packing).

If you are older or have recently become disabled and are looking at new equipment, you should first consider conventional tools that may be longer, lighter or have better handles before purchasing expensive gadgets and tools with limited use.

WEEDING

Traditional tools and methods

Probably the most common method of weeding is to crouch down and remove the weeds by hand or with a small fork or trowel. A far more efficient method practised by professional and amateur horticulturists alike is hoeing.

The two most commonly used tools are the draw hoe and the Dutch hoe. A two-handed chopping motion is needed when using the draw hoe, while the Dutch hoe can, to some extent, be used with one hand.

The main disadvantage of hoeing is that it has little effect on deep rooted weeds such as dandelions. It also requires a reasonable level of skill in crowded areas. This is probably why many people prefer to bend down and use small hand tools.

General tips to cut down weeding

- Plant your borders densely so that there is less opportunity for weeds to grow.
- Weed more frequently for shorter periods, ie five minutes every day will achieve more than one 35-minute session a week.
- Consider using a mulch, and temporarily cover open areas with cardboard, straw, grass clippings or carpet.

Alternative tools for easier weeding

A good technique for easy weeding involves using two tools: first, a more modern hoe for shallow-rooted weeds complemented by a specially designed tool for those that are deep rooted. The advantage of this method is that it is possible to deal with all your weeding without bending at all and, if necessary, with one hand.

A selection of such tools is listed below.

Wilkinson Sword Swoe (cultivator)

This is probably the easiest to use and most efficient gardening tool available today.

Its unique head design with three cutting edges makes the Swoe suitable for hoeing, taking out seed drills, weeding and earthing up. The steel golf-club-like head slides through the soil just below the surface taking out the roots of any weeds.

Unlike the draw hoe the Swoe (1.5m long and weighing 680g) cuts on both the forward and backward strokeand does not need to be lifted. The shaft is lightweight alloy and the handle has a plastic contoured grip for comfort. (Supplier: Wilkinson Sword)

Wilkinson Sword Swoe

Baronet weedpuller

Tried and tested for many years, this tool is made from rust-resistant steel with cadmium-plated blade and claw. It is designed to remove most weeds in cultivated soil but not in lawns or compacted ground.

The steel blade is pushed into the ground beside the weed and, when the trigger is squeezed, the claw grips the weed ready to pull it out. It is designed for one-handed use and greatly reduces the need

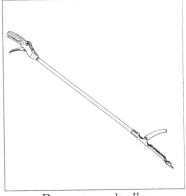

Baronet weedpuller

to bend down. However, the grip is not suitable for people with severe arthritic conditions of the hand and sthe safety catch can also be difficult for anyone with reduced dexterity.

The Baronet (864mm long and weighing 450g) is particularly suitable for someone working from a wheelchair and also for people of average height or less who are unable to bend. (Supplier: A Wright & Son)

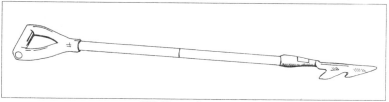

Wolf weed extractor

Weed extractor

To use this tool, the harpoon-like point is first pushed into the soil alongside the weed and then twisted round once or twice to loosen the roots and entangle the leaves round the barbs. The weed is then extracted by pulling on the D-grip handle.

This tool (1m long and weighing 500g) can be used on soil and lawn, and again you do not need to bend. Nor do you need a strong grip or particularly good dexterity. It is not very suitable for wheelchair users but can be used with one arm. (Supplier: Wolf-Tools)

Weedkey

The Weedkey consists of an enamelled steel tube with a T-bar handle which has moulded PVC grips at each end and three steel spikes at the bottom.

The tool (920mm long and weighing 1.1kg) is pushed into the ground above the weed and rotated once or twice to entangle the spikes in the leaves. The weed is then pulled out of the ground and ejected from the spikes by depressing the plunger at the top of the handle.

It does work on soil and lawns but leaves a large hole. This can be filled in by ejecting the plug containing the weed and inserting it into the hole upside down.

Two hands are needed to use this tool, but you do not have to bend. (Suppliers: Parasene - via New Waves Marketing; Standard Manufacturing Co)

Patio weeders

These tools are available from many manufacturers and are often described as 'weeding knives'. Designed for uprooting weeds from awkward crevices between paving slabs and in rock gardens, the scraper has a thin, sharp blade which is hooked under the weed to pull it out.

All the interchangeable ranges (Fiskars (UK), Erin-Gardena, Spear & Jackson and Wolf-Tools) include this tool and it can therefore be fitted to a range of handle lengths.

If you want a separate, fixed-head version, the tool described below is recommended. Patio weeders are suitable for most gardeners including wheelchair users. They can be used with one hand with practice.

Telescopic patio weeding knife

The DP 360 (extending from 820mm to 1.2m and weighing 300g) has a light aluminium handle with a soft foam grip and, as the inside edge has been sharpened, is also useful for cutting briars and nettles.

This tool is not interchangeable but is more comfortable to use than the other patio weeders. It is suitable for wheelchair users but two hands are

Telescopic patio weeding knife

needed to adjust the length. (Supplier: Darlac Products)

Gardena combisystem

This system consists of a range of
handles and toolheads which can be
interchanged to suit your
requirements. Wolf-Tools, Fiskars
(UK) and Spear and Jackson also
produce similar equipment, all
requiring two hands to fit and
detach.

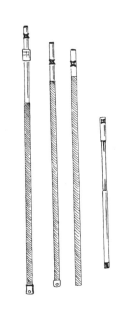

The Gardena system is unique in
that only one hand is needed to
change the toolheads. This is
particularly important if, for
example, you have had a stroke or
have injured one arm.

The best handle is the long
aluminium one (1.3m and weighing
300g) which can be cut down with a
hacksaw to make it more
manageable for raised bed users.

Gardena combisystem

The short handle (780mm and
weighing 100g) is liable to break if
it is subjected to heavy use or
abuse.

Hand grubber with weeder

For weeding, an excellent toolhead
for the combisystem handle is the
hand grubber with weeder. It has a
dual purpose: loosening and
aerating the soil with the prongs,
and weeding with the attached

Hand grubber with weeder

blade on the back. The steel toolhead is small and light (70mm working width and weighing 100g) and therefore suitable for people with reduced strength. (Supplier: Erin-Gardena)

Wolf multichange system

Like the above mentioned Gardena system, the Wolf multichange system consists of a range of handles and toolheads which can be interchanged to save space because there are less handles to store.

The tools are very robust and made of high quality materials. However, you need two strong hands to change the toolheads. A few are suitable for weeding.

Handles range from 160mm to 1.4 metres long and larger telescopic versions are available. (Supplier: Wolf-Tools)

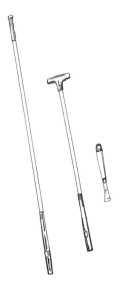

Wolf multichange system

Scuffle hoe

A good toolhead for the multichange handle, this double-edged weeding tool (160mm working width and weighing 300g) has a thin, sharp, serrated blade which cuts off annual weeds at ground level when pushed back and forth across the soil surface.
(Supplier: Wolf-Tools)

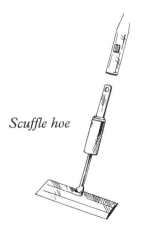

Scuffle hoe

Push-pull weeder

Push-pull weeder

The push-pull weeder (working width 150mm, head weighing 300g) is similar to the scuffle hoe but with side guards which reduce the risk of damage when it is too close to plants.

Weed Wand

This tool is better described as a long-handled blow torch which is used to burn weeds briefly so that they die. The weeds can then be more easily removed with other tools such as a patio knife, or burnt away completely a couple of days later when they have shrivelled and died.

The long handle (770mm) and light weight (900g) means it can be used easily with one hand and without bending. People with loss of sensation or co-ordination should not use it. (Supplier: Parasene via New Waves Marketing)

Weed Wand

Ground cover fabric - Permealay

This black, permeable fabric (1.5m wide x 6m long) can be used to control weeds either on open soil or under a range of crops, such as strawberries, currants and gooseberries. Crops may be planted through crosses cut in the Permealay, or, with existing crops, strips may be laid either side and stapled on both sides of each plant.

In addition to weed suppression, Permealay will conserve moisture and should reduce damage caused by a number of insect pests which overwinter in the soil under the bushes and trees. (Supplier: Agralan)

DIGGING AND CULTIVATING

Digging and cultivating seem to cause able bodied, older and disabled gardeners alike many problems. This is hardly surprising when you consider the ergonomics of digging in conjunction with the design of the human anatomy.

First, a large, heavy tool is thrust into the ground, then the soil is raised from below ground level before being flipped over and smashed to pieces and spread out level again. During this process a whole number of minor injuries can occur to the back, neck and shoulders.

To begin with, the thrusting of the fork can cause jarring and sprains to the wrist; the lifting element often causes lumber problems and, during the turning and dropping of the soil, the wrists can again be strained, and the spinal column can be subjected to damaging torsonal stresses that extend to the neck and shoulders.

The breaking up and levelling element may be the least demanding part of the process, but can still stretch and fatigue the muscles. Also, during a half-hour session the muscles may be forced to repeat the same actions a great many times - something that would challenge a dedicated fitness fanatic.

It is no wonder that tool inventors are constantly looking for an alternative to the fork and spade.

Traditional tools

Most forks and spades are too short for today's gardeners, as people's average height has increased since Victorian times, while the length of traditional tools has not. If you are able to dig and are determined to do so, then the first option is a longer fork.

Most alternatives, which can be described as gadgets and gizmos, disappear with the test of time. Below are some tried and tested alternatives.

But first, let us consider some useful tips.

General tips to make digging easier

- First, try a smaller tool, and/or longer tool; even consider a long-handled hand fork.
- Try an auxiliary handle on your existing fork or spade.
- Think about which element of the digging process causes you problems and modify your technique, for example, do not turn the soil but throw it forwards.
- Design your borders or vegetable patch in strips to minimise walking and compacting the soil.

Alternative tools for digging

New generation forks and spades

These moderately priced tools follow the traditional style but are lighter, longer and ergonomically designed to reduce strain. Strong and durable, they are available in two sizes - standard (1.1m long and weighing 1.9kg) and large (1.2m long and

Spade with auxiliary handle

weighing 2kg) with extra long, curved shafts for extra leverage.

A popular choice for the more able gardener, this may be the cheapest and easiest way to extend your digging activities, especially when combined with an auxiliary handle. (Suppliers: Spear and Jackson - Backsaver Range; Fiskars(UK) - Wilkinson Sword Power Range

The spades are similar.

Ergolite fork and spade

These are like the the Wilkinson Power range but are shorter and have a metal pear-shaped shaft so that they are lighter (1.65kg) and easier to grip. The same tools, known as the Ergowood range, are available with wooden pear-shaped shafts. (Supplier: Fiskars (UK))

Long-handled hand fork

Used like a full size tool, except that your feet are not used to push it in, this tool (overall length 1.4m and weighing 500g) is designed for small areas and to minimise bending. Users with only one arm can add the Peta add-on handle and arm support to give them extra power, more control and to reduce strain. (Supplier: Fiskars (UK))

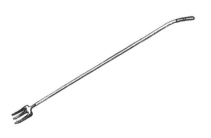

Long-handled hand fork

Medium-handled forks and trowels

These have the same features as the above tools except that they are shorter (950mm) and lighter (425g) which makes them easier to handle and transport. (Supplier: Wilkinson Sword)

Stainless steel long-handled garden fork and trowel

These tools (1.1m overall length) are similar to the Wilkinson medium length range except that they are lighter (380g) with a stainless steel finish and with a cranked handle for extra leverage.

As with many tools, the fact that they are lighter means that they are not quite as strong but this should not be a problem for most careful users. (Supplier: Ivyline)

Lightweight plastic handtools

For use in soft soil, tubs and containers, these very strong plastic forks and trowels are extremely light (50g). When combined with a pistol grip and arm support, these are the easiest and lightest tools to use for digging small areas. (Supplier: Fiskars (UK))

Small pistol-grip tools

The Peta range of garden tools consists of a fork, trowel, weeder, hoe and cultivator (overall length 150mm and weighing 100g).

All the metal parts are stainless steel which does not rust and reduces soil adhesion. The handles are at approximately 90 degrees from the toolhead so that the wrist and hand can be held in a stress-free position which enables the gardener to grip the tool more firmly.

Gardeners with weak hands or wrists will benefit considerably if they use a Peta arm support cuff, which plugs into the rear of any tool and can be changed from

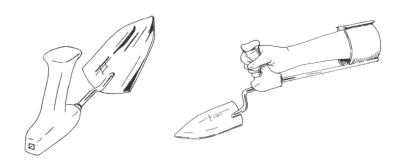

Short trowel   *Short trowel with arm support*

one tool to another. The strength of the forearm is then employed to assist the hand and wrist.

Long-reach pistol-grip tools

These are designed for gardeners who prefer to sit on a stool or chair while working. The tools (approximately 760mm long and weighing 430g) include a fork, trowel, cultivator and hoe. These long tools must be used with the interchangeable arm support to give greater control over the tool and reduce any strain on the wrist.

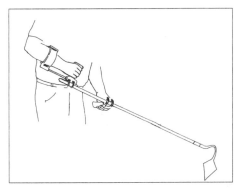

Arm support for long-reach pistol-grip tools

Arm support for pistol-grip tools

To give more power and control, especially on the long-reach versions, the arm support plugs into a slot at the back of the tool and can be taken out again to use on other Peta tools. The standard cuff is made of hard plastic similar to that on a crutch. A softer Velcro version is available. Bear in mind that you will need another free hand to do up the Velcro. (Supplier: Peta (UK))

Auxiliary handles

On full size and border forks and spades, these D-grips can be fitted halfway up the shaft to reduce bending and make it possible for the gardener to adopt a more comfortable posture. The plastic handles are cheaper and lighter (100g) than the meta ones (300g), but are harder to fit. (Supplier: Peta UK - plastic D-grip add-on handle; Wolf-Tools - metal D-grip handle)

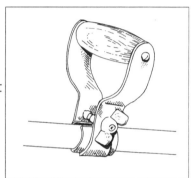

Auxiliary handle

Pistol-grip add-on handle

Wheelchair users and people with one arm using long-handled tools, such as a long-handled hand fork, will benefit from using the Peta add-on handle (weighing 50g) with arm support.

The pistol grip provides a safe and comfortable grip while the arm support increases control and leverage which is essential on longer tools. (Supplier: Peta UK)

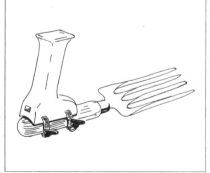

Short fork with plastic pistol-grip add-on handle

Alternatives to forks and spades

Wolf Soil Miller

If you are unable to use a traditional fork or spade, do not despair. The Wolf Soil Miller is like a miniature plough that, with the right adaptations, can be used, one-handed and without bending, to cultivate open soil.

Wolf Soil Miller

Popular with allotment holders and vegetable growers, this tool (150mm working width, toolhead weighing 1.4kg) will dig down about 100mm in light soil and leave the soil with a fine tilth ready for planting.

Moving backwards and forwards through the soil, the star wheels break down lumps, and the rocking pendulum blade cuts off weeds and controls the depth of work down to 100mm.

On light soils it is a useful alternative to digging where deep cultivation is unnecessary or digging impractical. It can also be used to mix in manure or compost which has been spread over the surface. It is a

Garden Claw

heavy tool, but can be wheeled into position and need not be lifted off the ground.

The best handle length is 1.4m and, fitted with the Peta add-on handle and arm support, the Wolf Soil

Miller can be used with one arm and by people with mild arthritic conditions. (Supplier: Wolf-Tools)

Garden Claw

The Garden Claw is ideal for loosening and aerating soil. The long handle (1m) means that the gardener has no need to bend. This tool (weighing 1.8kg) will also uproot many types of weeds, and can be used for turning your compost heap, digging in manure or fertiliser and as a lawn aerator.

A smaller version is designed for use with one hand, but this is not recommended for anyone with any type of upper limb problem. (Suppliers: Joseph Enterprises UK; Spear and Jackson)

PRUNING

Cutting branches and stems

Traditional tools

The common problems associated with these tools — anvil or bypass pruners (secateurs), loppers, saws — is their weight and the amount of strength required to use them. Also, the safety catches on pruning tools can be very awkward to use.

Alternative tools for pruning

The main features of the alternatives are longer handles to improve access and reduce bending and the provision of some form of power gain by using ratchets or by gearing through pulleys.

Smaller, lighter pruners are also available.

Darlac Snapper

The reasonably lightweight (350g and 650mm long) Short Snapper will collect as it cuts, making it ideal for light pruning and dead-heading in difficult-to-reach areas such as rose arches and pergolas. With a 360 degree swivel head, Snapper is ideal for gathering fruit beyond your grasp, and it is of great value when dealing with prickly plants such as holly.

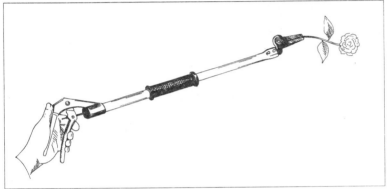

Darlac Snapper

It can also be used to pick up severed branches and place them in the barrow. The fact that it can be operated with one hand makes it invaluable for wheelchair gardeners, and the 1 metre model (the Long Snapper, weighing 400g) is the most practical to reduce the amount of bending for ambulant gardeners. (Supplier: Darlac Products)

Ratchet pruners

These cheaply priced secateurs with a ratchet action cut cleanly through stems up to 20mm in diameter with minimal effort The plastic handles are strong and light and the hardened steel blade is coated to resist corrosion and is easily cleaned.

The method of opera-
tion requires some thought
and practice but is well
worth the effort. These are
the easiest pruners to use
and also the lightest (96g)
and cheapest.

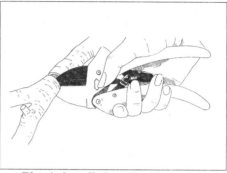

The jaws are placed
well over the stem and the
handles squeezed until
resistance is felt. Pressure is

Plastic handled ratchet pruners

then released so that the ratchet makes a clicking sound.
This light squeezing and releasing action is repeated up
to four times, depending on the thickness of the stem,
until the cut is completed. Very thin stems may be cut
through with the first squeeze.

Attempting to cut
through thicker stems
with one squeeze may
damage the ratchet
mechanism. A wire loop
closes the secateur when
not in use.

This secateur is
recommended for people
with weak grip or arth-
ritic fingers. (Suppliers:
Ceka Tools; Spear and
Jackson)

Cut and grip secateurs

Heavy duty ratchet pruners

These pruners (weighing 100g) are similar to the ratchet
pruners described above but are of a better quality and
have a slightly wider cutting diameter. (Supplier: Ceka
Tools)

Cut and grip secateurs

After cutting through the branch or stem, the pruners (weighing 200g) then hold onto it so that it easy to remove. This prevents the stem from dropping onto the ground so that it has to be picked up again. It is an ideal tool for someone with one arm and reduces the need to bend. (Supplier: Wolf-Tools)

Long-reach pruning for higher branches

For reaching into the highest branches of trees, a number of tools can reduce the need to use a ladder. The longer the tool the more strength will be required and, generally, two strong arms are a necessity.

Telescopic handle for branch pruners and saws

Telescopic handles, branch pruners and saws

These tools can be acquired from many manufactures, including two of the interchangeable ranges — Wolf and Gardena. The easiest to use are the ones with a hook-type blade to hang over the branch before cutting

Branch pruners with 4-fold transmission

These pruners (up to 5m long and weighing 2kg — including the handle) are easy to operate since they incorporate an energy-saving 4-fold transmission and wide-opening blade. They have a hardened, non-stick coated blade which ensures a smooth,

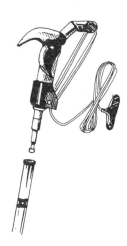

Branch pruner with 4-fold transmission

clean cut. The tough cord (4.7m long) has a small plastic handle grip. They are recommended for the combisystem telescopic handles for up to 5 metres working height.

Combisystem gardener's saw

This saw (360mm overall length and weighing 100g) cuts branches up to 5m when fitted to the combisystem telescopic handle. It complements the branch pruner and can also be fitted to the smallest handle and used on small branches as an alternative to pruners. (Supplier: Erin-Gardena)

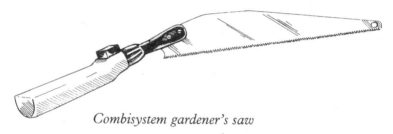

Combisystem gardener's saw

Note: Wolf-Tools produces a similar system — but you need two hands to exchange the heads and more co-ordination when using the pruners.

Garden saws

These tools are specially designed with wide open teeth for cutting live green wood. There is a wide range of sizes and styles. For any gardener the folding type is safer and easier to carry. Fixed blade saws should be stored and moved in a scabbard.

A number of companies make small folding saws. A saw can be easier to use on small branches and stems than a large pair of pruners. One of the best designed is described below.

Small folding saw

This is the smallest (160mm),
lightest (50g) and easiest to carry
multi-purpose saw. The safety
lock is simple to manage. The
saw is designed to cut on the pull
stroke which makes it easier to
use. (Supplier: Gardena (UK))

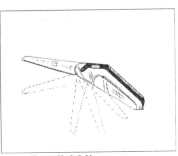

Small folding saw

Trimming grass and soft foliage

Traditional tools and methods

The most common tools are the heavy, two-handled
shears that often jar the user's joints and cause the
muscles to become overstretched. More sophisticated
gardeners may also have two pairs of long-handled
shears for the lawn, one for side edges and one for the
flat edges; both these tools are frequently too short so
that the gardener, who has to stoop down to use them,
may suffer backpain.

Tips to make cutting and trimming easier

- Reduce complicated shapes in your lawn and have less
  corners.
- Design your lawn so that it adjoins, and is slightly
  higher than, a hard edge (for example, of a path) so
  that you can mow over the edge.
- Plant slower growing or evergreen shrubs that produce
  less foliage.

Alternative tools for trimming grass and soft foliage

(See also Lawn care, page 62.)

One-handed shears

These shears (120mm long and weighing 300g) are designed for softer foliage and grass. The best models have blades that can be swivelled through 180 degrees to cut into the vertical surfaces so that you do not have to rotate your arm.

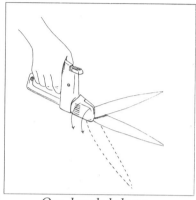

One-handed shears

If you can bend, kneel or sit, they can be used on the lawn. They are often used to trim soft hedging like heathers and rockery plants. The safety catches on Wolf and Gardena are the easiest to use. Care should be taken with one-handed shears if you have arthritic hands.

Electric shears may be a better option if you have good balance and co-ordination. (Suppliers: Fiskars (UK) and Darlac - *only non-electric shears*); Erin-Gardena; Wolf-Tools)

Sheep shears

Also known as the Multi-shears, this lightweight (150g — overall length 250mm) trimming tool for one-handed use is based on the old principle of the sheep shears. These shears have 100mm long blades of high quality carbon steel which retain their sharp cutting edge indefinitely. The spring steel handle is hard but comfortable to hold and requires only a light grip.

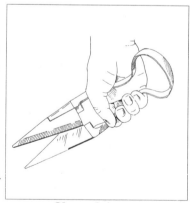

Sheep shears

The blades are gently squeezed together for cutting and open automatically when pressure is released. This is basically an old fashioned alternative to the one-handed shears mentioned above. (Supplier: Burgeon and Ball)

Long-handled, lightweight lawn shears

These lawn-edging shears (weighing 1.2kg) have extra long (990mm) aluminum handles to reduce bending. The shears have rust resistant blades and the handles have cushioning rubber grips to combat the effect of jarring. The blade (185mm long) is adjusted with a self-locking wing nut. (Suppliers: Ceka Tools; Damar International)

Useful tip: You may be able to extend the length of your existing lawn shears by riveting aluminum-tubed extensions to the handles. Use foam pipe lagging to create a soft grip.

Electric shears with extension

Electric shears with extensions

These cordless, battery-powered shears run for approximately 40 to 60 minutes and have a 80mm cutting width. They can be used with one hand and are suitable for stems up to 4mm in diameter (more if they are softer). A safety switch prevents accidental start-up. They are sold with an external charging unit, and can be recharged 500 times or more frequently.

To save bending, an extension handle can be fitted to some models. The Wolf extension handle has small wheels for easier use. The Gardena models can also edge the lawn if the handle is turned through 90 degrees. (Suppliers: Wolf-Tools; Erin-Gardena; Black and Decker)

Ultralight shears

These ultralight shears (600g and 160mm long) are based on traditional shears but, as their name suggests, are much lighter. They have stainless steel and strong alloy handles. Two arms are needed to use this tool and, like all similar shears, it can cause jarring to delicate joints. (Supplier: Darlac Products)

Ultralight shears

Cordless electric hedge trimmer

This small, lightweight (900g) hedge trimmer is powered by rechargeable batteries that can also be used in other garden and DIY products such as a strimmer, drill, and screwdriver.

The safety catch prevents accidental use but does require some dexterity. It is a very effective and convenient tool for small jobs. The fact that it does not having a cable is also a safety bonus. (Supplier: Black and Decker)

WATERING

Watering, which is the preoccupation of many gardeners and the bane of their lives, is the most easily solved

problem for elderly and disabled gardeners. Britain is a
world leader in irrigation systems and, if you are
prepared, or are able, to spend enough money, all can be
done at the touch of a button. For most of us something
less technical will suffice.

Traditional tools

The best known watering tool is the round metal
watering can which must be held away from your body
to prevent it from bruising your legs. This causes
excessive strain and twisting of the spine especially when
someone is reaching out to water. In addition, the effort
involved in constantly raising the arm up and down to
control the water flow can involve strenuous effort when
the can is full.

However, before considering alternative equipment, a
number of things can be done to reduce or eliminate the
task.

Tips to cut down watering

• *Cultivate drought resistant plants*
As a general rule, plants with silvery foliage are generally
more drought resistant, eg lavender, senecio and stachis.
Aromatic plants and waxy leaved plants, such as
rosemary, thyme, geraniums, rue and sedums, also
tolerate hot, dry conditions For more details, consult a
plant encyclopaedia (see Appendix 3, Further reading).
• *Mulching*
Spreading a layer of wood-bark, gravel, well-rotted
manure or organic material will help the soil to retain
moisture. If you do have to water, remember to add
extra water to take account of this material or fit
watering tubes near key plants. Mulching also has the
benefit that it suppresses weeds.

- *Use the 'no-dig' or 'low-dig' technique* (see p 3.)
Because the soil is disturbed less often if you use this
technique, less moisture will be lost from the soil in the
summer months.
- *Use silicon gels in containers and baskets*
Bought in packets and looking like sugar, these silicon
crystals swell up when water is added and turn into a
jelly-like mass so that more moisture is retained in the
soil. As the moisture is released the crystals shrink; and,
on further watering, they swell up again. This method is
ideal for tubs and containers and for use in very dry
beds.

Alternative equipment for watering

Narrow profile plastic cans

The advantage of a thin, rectangular,
5-litre watering can is that you can
hold it closer to your body and so
adopt a better posture and subject
yourself to less strain. Plastic is also
lighter and less likely to bruise your
legs. For people with back problems
it may be worth carrying two smaller
watering cans to distribute the strain
more evenly (ie one in each hand).
(Suppliers: Geeco; Harcoaster;
Hozelock; Plysu)

Narrow profile plastic can

Watermatic can

This controllable 5-litre can allows
the gardener to water with speed
and accuracy — from a small trickle
for the smallest seedlings to a full

Watermatic can

flow for larger plants. It has a unique, patented valve system that does not clog. An extension spout makes it possible to water more inaccessible plants and, if the gardener rests the spout on the ground, he or she will not have to bend. (Supplier: Harcoaster)

Using a hosepipe

Tips on how to use hosepipes

- It is best to use an outside tap but it must be fitted with a non-return valve (this is a legal requirement to stop dirty water siphoning back into the mains).
- If you leave your hosepipe out, keep it raised to your level by attaching it to hooks on the wall.
- Use corner guides to prevent snagging on walls and other objects.
- Split the hose into sections to create stations using waterstop connectors (see diagram below).
- Use seep or sprinkler hoses, especially on the areas which are furthest away.
- Use hose-end feeders for fertilizer and pesticides.

Moving and storing your hosepipe

The usual problem with hosepipes is that they become entagled, heavy with water and trip people up. If you like to put your hosepipe away frequently, then you will need some form of reel. Many are available, but one of the most interesting rewinds itself automatically.

Retracta auto-rewind hose

This hose reel (18m long) rewinds itself automatically when a catch is released on the reel. Mounted on a wall bracket, the reel swings through 180 degrees and can be folded flat against a wall when not in use.

The advantage for disabled gardeners is that they never have to rewind the hose manually. This hose has been successfully tried at tested at the Mary Marlborough Centre. (Supplier: Redashe)

Advanced hosepipe use - watering stations

If you find it difficult or even dangerous to drag a hosepipe around the garden, a technique used at the Mary Marlborough Centre involves leaving your hosepipe out and carrying only the spray gun to conveniently placed 'watering stations'.

At each station, waterstop connectors allow you to break into the system without getting wet or having to go back and turn the water off.

Once you have finished watering from that station, the hose is reconnected and you move on to the next station. This technique is quick and easy to use and requires little strength since the only thing you carry is a small plastic spray gun

It is also possible, if you find it difficult to bend, to raise the hosepipe to your level at the watering stations by hanging it on a hook screwed to the wall or tree. Tie some string to the pipe and hang it up.

At each station you can also use a lawn sprinkler or hose-end feeder to apply liquid fertilizer such as Phosphogen or Miracle Gro.

Spray guns

A vast number of spray guns is available. One of the easiest to use is the Hozelock model 2667

Watering stations

which comes with a detachable rose head, is very light, uncomplicated and can be operated with one hand.

Watering lances

A number of companies manufacture lightweight, rigid extension tubes which can be attached to the end of your hosepipe to provide extra reach and also enable you to turn the water on and off where you are working. Most models are approximately 850mm in length with the exception of the Darlac extendible lance described below.

Extendible watering lance

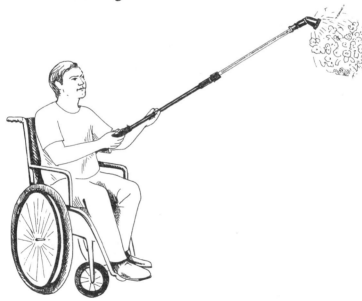

Extendible watering lance

This watering lance (weighing 180g) is telescopic (780mm - 1.3m), comes with a rose on the end, and has an easy-to-use on/off switch. (Supplier: Darlac Products)

Hose-end feeders

Hose-end feeders are spray guns with a plastic bottle attached to hold liquid chemicals for feeding plants and lawns. One is the Miracle Gro dispenser. (Suppliers: Miracle Garden Care; Hozelock; Phosphogen)

Timers and computers

Water computer (operated by buttons) on outside tap *Electronic water timer*

These devices are fitted to your tap and used to turn the water on and off to a pre-set volume or for a period of time. Their advantage for an older gardener or gardener with disabilities is primarily as a labour saving technique. Also, because the electronic timers already contain a valve, they do not require an external non-return valve to prevent back syphoning.

Setting up your timer will require a little patience and some models are very 'fiddly'. The Hozelock battery operated electronic timer can be programmed to turn your water on and off up to four times a day and can be manually overridden. (Suppliers: Agriframes; Erin-Gardena; Hozelock)

MOVING AND HANDLING

How equipment and other materials can be moved around the garden is the main focus of this section, but other items of equipment to make life easier for older gardeners and gardeners with disabilities are also considered.

Traditional tools for moving materials and equipment

The heavy wooden or galvanised barrow with one wheel at the front and two handles at the back has, for many years, been a favourite piece of gardening equipment. However, even if you have two strong arms and legs, losing your balance and tipping over while using it are distinct possibilities.

Alternative kinds of wheelbarrow

In the past many companies have produced wheelbarrows or garden trucks aimed specifically at older gardeners and gardeners with disabilities. Unfortunately, most of these are no longer being produced. Wheelchair users will find it difficult to move any wheelbarrow except on an even surface.

Trailer Barrow

Trailer Barrow

This is a robust barrow for smaller gardens which can be used with one hand. It has puncture-proof tyres and its large capacity can be increased with extension sides. It has a high quality plastic body. (Supplier: Trailer Barrow Co)

Garden Twin

This is a galvanized metal wheelbarrow with two large balloon tyres at the front and a pram-type handle at the rear which makes it possible for someone with with one arm to use it. Despite being quite heavy, it is very stable and easy to manoeuvre. (Supplier: Haemerlin Products)

Ascender lift barrow

The galvanized steel bin of this wheelbarrow (weighing 18kg) can be lowered to the ground by rotating it using the two tubular steel handles. Heavy and bulky items can be loaded at ground level, and weeds and leaves can be raked up or swept directly into the barrow without stooping or using other tools.

The bin is returned to the conventional position by levering back on the handles until they automatically lock into place. There is a locking lever on each side of the barrow, both of which operate the release mechanism.

Two friction rollers under the bin enable it to be wheeled along in the lowered position. The barrow can be upended in the lowered position to take up less space when not in use. The wheel of the barrow has a pneumatic rubber tyre. (Supplier: Allan Power Equipment)

Easy Roller Lawn Cart

This is a strong, lightweight and manoeuvrable cart made of plastic with a steel axle. There are tool clips on

the side and a recessed tray for carrying tools. Because
of its wide wheelbase and flat bottom, this cart has good
overall stability. (Supplier: Agriframes)

Adapted trolley

Adapted trolley

Because of the lack of commercially available options,
many people decide to adapt an existing trolley to suit
their own requirements. Golf trolleys, tea trolleys and
anything with wheels may be suitable. If you are unable
to design or build something yourself to transport your
tools and materials, an organisation called REMAP, run
by retired engineers, makes one-off customised items for
people with disabilities.

Wheelchair caddies

These are plastic fold-down brackets that attach to the
front of a wheelchair. They can be used to support a
box, bag or tools laid horizontally across the brackets.
Manufactured in California by Quickie, they are quite
expensive but indispensable for active wheelchair users.
An innovative person with some DIY skills could make
something similar from a pair of shelving brackets.
(Supplier: GBL Wheelchairs)

Tool caddies

Some caddies can be used to
carry tools and garden
rubbish while others only
hold a bag. Manufactured by
various companies, these
items look like a cross
between a golf bag and a bin-
bag holder. None are suitable
for wheelchair users because
they need to be tipped onto
two wheels to be moved.
Also, ambulant disabled
people should not use these
caddies for support like a
walking frame as they are not
particularly stable. (Suppliers:
Erin-Gardena; Hoselock)

Tool caddy

Garden truck

For moving heavy, awkward
loads, this multi-purpose
truck can be used upright
like sack wheels or as a four-
wheeled horizontal truck for
larger, heavier loads.

It has a tough frame
made of steel and come
with a dustbin bag holder
for garden rubbish.
(Supplier: Black &
Decker)

Garden truck

Other useful items of equipment

Toolbelts and aprons

Ambulant older gardeners or gardeners with disabilies
are recommended to wear belts, aprons and even jackets
with lots of pockets so that they carry string, pruners,
dibbers, knives, small trowels with them as they move
about the garden. This will cut down on the endless time
and energy spent trailing back to the garden shed.

Toolbelts are not suitable for wheelchair users but a
sleeveless fishing jacket with big pockets may be
appropriate. (Supplier: Spear and Jackson)

Kneeler stools

Kneeler stools

These small stools can be used for sitting on or can be
turned upside down and knelt on. If the stool is turned
upside down, the legs become supports to help you get
up and down. They are available in metal or plastic.

The Easy Kneeler Stool (weighing 4.3kg) has a stove-
enamelled tubular steel frame and a wooden seat with a
separate plastic cushion. The height of the seat
(510mm)and the well-shaped handles make it suitable

for gardeners who have difficulty getting up from a low seat. The kneeler platform is 75mm above the ground. (Supplier: JB Corrie & Co)

The Croydex Kneeler Seat (430mm high and weighing 2.3kg) is made from durable and weatherproof lightweight plastic. The fact that the handles on all four corners extend beyond the seat area not only make it less likely to tilt on soft ground but also easy to carry. The seat is raised 45mm above the ground when used as a kneeler. The pad should be assembled facing the side most appropriate to the user's needs as it is difficult to dismantle at a later date. (Supplier: Croydex)

Knee pads and kneeling mats

If you undertake a lot of work while kneeling, then some form of protection on hard surfaces is recommended, especially if you have skin or circulation problems. The advantage of knee pads is that they are always in place but they can be uncomfortable. Some are made of foam and others have canvas covers.

Kneeling mats have to be moved about but, on the other hand, you can also sit on them. They are also made from high density foam. Both items are widely available from high street shops and by mail order.

Jay active cushion

This is a small (250 x 120mm), silicon-filled, medical cushion commonly used by those taking part in disabled sporting activities, such as sailing, to prevent pressure sores. The cushion can be used like a kneeler pad or sat on. A harness which enables the cushion to be worn around the wearer's bottom is available and can be useful if someone needs to move around on the ground. (Supplier: GBL Wheelchairs)

Grabber rake

This plastic leaf rake works like a squeegee to pick up leaves and other debris after raking. A two-in-one tool, it is useful if you have trouble bending. (Supplier: Blackwall Products)

Leaf grabber

The leaf grabber is another tool which enables you to pick up material without bending. At least four models are available. The weight and length of these varies but the Supagrab model (900mm long and weighing 800g) has been the most popular at the Mary Marlborough Centre. (Supplier: Standard Manufacturing)

Leaf grabber

Lightweight yard broom

While most garden brooms are over 300mm wide and are quite heavy, the nylon Victory deck broom is only 180mm wide and weighs 200g, making it much easier to handle. The plastic head has a screw-in fitting to take an aluminium handle available from most hardware shops. (Supplier: Victory)

The Helping Hand

This is a long-handled (350mm) grabbing tool for picking up hard-to-reach debris in the garden. The more common version has one moving claw and is suitable for picking up smaller items. The more advanced, the Arthri-grip, can be used for gripping a wider variety of items, including small pots up to 9mm in diameter. (Supplier: Helping Hand Company)

The Helping Hand

Portapath

To provide access on soft or unstable ground, the Portapath (standard roll 3m x 900mm) is made by linking together small sections (300 x 70 x 20mm thick) of Polypropylene to form a platform or a length of track. Sections can be snapped together to form paths of different lengths and widths. For example, a series of single sections makes a narrow track

One section of the Portapath

(300mm wide) which is suitable for a wheelbarrow or to walk on; two sections wide (600mm) will accommodate a walking frame, and three sections (900mm wide) a wheelchair The path can be rolled up for storage when not in use. It can also be left down permanently and will last many years. (Supplier: Newbrook Products)

LAWN CARE

The main piece of equipment used in lawn care is the mower and, while there are many solutions to the problems associated with this aspect of gardening for older and less disabled people, the options for wheelchairs users and those with more severe difficulties are limited.

Mowing all but the smallest lawn from a wheelchair is hardly realistic. This is one area of gardening where the best solution may be to recognise your limitations and seek help. 'High-tech', high-cost solutions like robotic solar powered mowers are available and may become more common in the future.

If you have a moderate mobility problem or reduced strength or stamina, then modern technology and design can come to your rescue at a reasonable cost.

Useful tips

- Construct a smaller, simpler lawn with fewer corners and borders.
- Create a mowing strip to reduce edging.
- Don't cut the lawn so short.
- Leave off the grass box in hot weather - this is not only labour saving but protects the grass from the sun and returns nutrients to the soil.
- Learn to appreciate daisies, buttercups and other 'lawn weeds'!

Mowers

Whether to buy a rotary or cylinder mower is the perennial question for all gardeners. The answer depends on the size of your lawn and the finish you require. Cylinder mowers produce the best finish but are not so efficient on long or damp grass. They are also more difficult to sharpen.

Rotary mowers come with wheels - except on the hover mower variety. Once started, the hover mower can be easy to move, but bear in mind that it will have to be carried to the lawn before mowing and carried back.

CREATE A SIMPLER LAWN WITH FEWER CORNERS AND BORDERS

Before

After

Whether to choose a petrol or electric mower is the next question. For smaller lawns an electric mower is more convenient as a lightweight model can be used. For very small lawns or lawns with patchy growth, a strimmer may be an alternative solution.

Safety note: All cable operated electric mowers and strimmers should be used only with an RCB (residual circuit breaker) which plugs into your electric socket and will prevent you from being electrocuted should the cable be cut.

Electric mowers

Rotary hover mowers

Flymo Micro Lite

The Micro Lite is a very lightweight (4.7kg) rotary hover mower without a grassbox. It has swing-back plastic safety blades and two cutting heights. One of the lightest mowers on the market, this flymo's main drawbacks are that you may have to rake up the grass clippings and, because it does not have wheels, you will have to carry it to and from the lawn. (Supplier: Flymo)

Hover mower with grassbox

For larger lawns the Micro-Compact 30 (7.5kg) hover mower has a 300mm cut and a grass collection box. It is heavier than the Micro Lite and comes with a plastic dura-blade or a metal blade. A spanner is needed to adjust the cutting height on a hover mower. (Supplier: Flymo)

Rotary wheeled mower with grassbox

These mowers are easy to use but cannot be moved
sideways like a hover. The main features to look out for
are: easy-to-use safety catches, grass boxes and a cutting
height adjustment. (Suppliers: Black and Decker;
Qualcast)

Electric cylinder mowers with grassbox

An additional benefit of these mowers is that the
Qualcast models can also be used to rake your lawn to
remove moss and thatch. The QX system involves
replacing the cylinder with another one which has tines
to rake out the debris. The QX system is available in
three sizes and the larger, more expensive Classic model
mowers are available with self propulsion. (Suppliers:
Black and Decker; Qualcast)

Battery mowers

These rotary wheeled mowers with a grassbox have
easily removable Ni-cad batteries; their height can easily
be adjusted and there is no cable to trip over. The Ni-
cad battery and an external mains charger are included
in the initial price. As battery technology improves, these
mowers are likely to become increasingly popular as they
are the easiest to use. Their relatively high price is their
main disadvantage. (Supplier: Wolf-Tools)

Petrol mowers

The advantage of petrol mowers is that they are usually
more powerful and so more appropriate for large lawns.
However, they are also heavier and, if you have any
mobility impairment, the only petrol mowers worth

LAWNMOWERS AND STRIMMERS

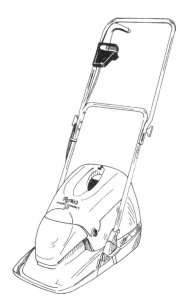

*Flymo Micro-Compact
hover mower*

Mini Trim strimmer

Rotary wheeled mower

*Electric cylinder mower with
grassbox removed*

having are probably the self-propelled versions, either cylinder or rotary.

Another problem is that considerable strength is needed to start them; and, even if you are strong, you can wrench your shoulder if you have not acquired the correct technique. Some of the more expensive models have the option of an electric start.

Petrol cylinder mowers

The advantage of these heavy mowers is that they are self-propelled; however, they do have a habit of running away with you. If you are agile and strong enough to be able to use one, be careful to check that it has an electric start and whether a scarifying cassette, such as that found on the Qualcast Balmoral, can be fitted.

Petrol rotary mowers

For rougher lawns these mowers are ideal, but only the more expensive models are self propelled and have the option of an electric start.

Strimmers

For small lawns, overgrown lawns and areas of long grass next to walls and around trees, a strimmer is a very useful tool. Most are powered by mains electricity and cut with a nylon cord.

Some models have the ability to cut the vertical edges of lawns and can therefore replace the traditional lawn edging shears. The more basic models are most efficient on flat areas.

Some of the lighter models can be used with one arm but have a smaller cutting capacity. Heavier duty models are now fitted with an auxiliary handle so that you can use them with two hands more comfortably with less bending.

Wheelchair users can use some lighter strimmers but they may put strain on the back.

A common problem with strimmers is that the nylon cord becomes jammed in its cartridge and is very difficult to remove. To avoid this, new models have been introduced which use a plastic clip-on blade instead of cord. When this breaks or wears out, it is simply pulled off and replaced.

Mini Trim

For cutting horizontally this small strimmer is available with the conventional nylon cord cartridge which can be difficult to replace. The advantages of this model are the wrist support and easy on-off button. (Supplier: Flymo)

Strimmer for cutting small lawns

This new style strimmer has a wide roller which moves easily and enables you to maintain an even cutting height. If you have a small or rough lawn and like the 'meadow style', then this tool could be an alternative to a mower. (Supplier: Wolf-Tools)

Cordless rechargeable strimmer

A cordless tool is easy to use and has the advantage that you can take it anywhere and there is no cable to trip over. The disadvantage is that the batteries will run down and need recharging. For small jobs the cordless tool is ideal. This model forms part of a range and the batteries can be used in other tools as well. The strimmer has plastic blades that are easy to change and it is very light. If you have a spare set of batteries, its working time can be doubled. (Supplier: Black and Decker)

Strimmer for edge cutting

By turning the handle round on the Revolution strimmer you will be able to cut the vertical edges of your lawn quite easily. As with many strimmers you will need some dexterity to use the safety catch on this model. (Suppliers: Flymo)

Traditional way to cut lawn edges

Long-handled lightweight lawn shears

These lawn-edging shears have extra long (990mm) aluminium handles so that you do not have to bend so much. The shears (weighing 1.2kg) have rust resistant, long blades (185mm) and the handles have cushioning rubber grips to combat the effect of jarring. The blades are adjusted by a self-locking wing nut. (See also p 47.) (Supplier: Ceka Tools)

Other lawn care tasks

Apart from mowing, lawn care — unless you want to achieve a 'meadow' effect — involves many other tasks.

Weeding, watering, scarifying, aerating, pest control and feeding are the main ones.

Weeding your lawn

Weeding can be undertaken in two ways: manually and by chemical control.

For manual weeding a number of tools and gadgets are available (see p 28).

Chemical control can be acheived by spraying the weedkiller from a watering-

Spreader for applyin
dry chemicals

can or hosepipe-end feeder, or by applying dry chemicals with a spreader. All methods have their advantages and disadvantages. Hose-end feeders are light and easy to use, but it can be difficult to judge how much is being applied. Using a spreader is better on large lawns, but take care not to overlap and double dose areas.

Feeding your lawn

To feed your lawn, you can employ similar methods. Indeed, some products claim to both weed and feed the lawn. Using these will therefore save you work.

Watering your lawn

Kew Gardens recommends weekly rather than daily watering. There are many ways to water your lawn; permanently installed pop-up sprinklers are the best, followed by a mobile lawn sprinkler and, lastly, a hosepipe.

Raking and scarifying your lawn

Scarifyers remove the debris and moss from your lawn. This can be a back-breaking task if you use a lawn rake. There are lightweight plastic rakes, but for any but the smallest areas the best solution is to use an electric scarifyer. Since this task is undertaken infrequently it may be better to hire one. (See also QX system p 66).

Be prepared for many bags of debris. (Suppliers: Qualcast; Black and Decker)

Aerating your lawn

In order to aerate the soil in the lawn many people use a garden fork to create the holes needed to allow air and fertiliser to get to the roots of the grass. Using a fork can compact the soil, however, and hole punchers which remove a plug of soil are therefore preferable.

The Wolf Multichange Hollow Tine Aerator is lightweight (300g and 220mm wide), ensures good drainage in problem lawn areas and creates soft-sided holes up to 60mm deep. It is designed to be used by pushing down with the foot, but it is possible to use it by pushing down with the arms. If you water the lawn before using this tool, it is easier to push into the soil. (Supplier: Wolf-Tools)

GREENHOUSES AND GARDEN FRAMES

Cedar-framed Alton greenhouse

A greenhouse enables gardeners to extend their activities into the winter and to cultivate a wider range of plants.

However, do not underestimate the cost and the amount of maintenance required to keep a greenhouse. Disabled gardeners particularly should bear this in mind, since they may need to buy the more expensive models with automated equipment.

As is the case with all gardening activities, there are cheaper ways of maintaining a greenhouse, but you will need to be innovative and have some DIY skills. In this book the usual options are considered, and those who want to pursue alternative methods are referred to other sources. A mail order company produces an excellent catalogue of greenhouse equipment (Two West's and Elliott). REMAP may be able to help with adaptations, and those who want more specialist advice should contact Horticultural Therapy or the Mary Marlborough Centre.

Greenhouses

Cedar greenhouses

An excellent greenhouse which should suit everyone including wheelchair users is the cedar-framed Alton greenhouse (3.2m long - sections can be added if required - and 2.3m wide) which is erected on a concrete plinth. It has a single sliding door with a clear opening of 760mm and no threshold. Cedar staging in different widths is available and side vents as well as roof vents are included in the design. Detachable timber cladding panels can be fitted to the lower part of the side walls to protect or replace the glass if desired.

For people at risk of falling, plastic sheets can be used instead of glass but they are very expensive.

A similar model (3m or 3.6m long and 2.7m wide) is produced by Parklines and has an even wider door (900mm) and fully adjustable shelving. (Suppliers: Alton; Parklines)

Aluminium greenhouses

Most aluminium greenhouses have a raised threshold

and small door which is very difficult to adapt for wheelchair users. However, Robinsons greenhouses have been designed with older people and people with disabilities in mind. Again, there is no door threshold to impede access.

The Royale range of greenhouses are 2.59m wide and available in a variety of lengths from 2.64m upwards. All have easily sliding, lockable, double doors. (Supplier: Robinsons)

Plastic greenhouses

An interesting option which is unusual to look at and relatively untested is a metal-framed greenhouse (4m wide — doors 2m wide — total length 2m upwards) covered in industrial strength bubblewrap. Possible advantages of this type are its safety and portability. Also, it would not be beyond the scope of someone who is good at DIY to make something similar using bed irons, angle irons or pressure treated timber. (Supplier: CLM Fabrications)

Equipment for greenhouses

Automatic vents

These moderately priced wax-filled openers will save you the trouble of opening and closing windows. Various models are available, including versions to open the lower louvre vents which, when combined with top-opening windows, provide the best airflow and ventilation. (Supplier: Jemp Engineering)

Wax-filled control for opening top windows automatically

Heating your greenhouse

Assuming that an electrical supply has been fitted in the greenhouse, a very easy heater to use is a thermostatically controlled fan heater. Oil-filled, electrically heated tubes are another option but they do not provide the same airflow as a fan heater. Paraffin heaters have obvious safety disadvantages besides being time consuming to fill and maintain.

Watering systems

The ideal greenhouse has its own water supply with two taps — one for a hosepipe and filling cans and the other for an automated watering system. The range of systems is enormous and varies from 'high-tech' to 'no-tech' (see Two West's and Elliott catalogue).

The systems using computers and drippers are versatile and effective but difficult to install and expensive.

Cheaper ways to water your greenhouse

- Connect a waterbutt to the guttering and run a hose off it into the greenhouse.

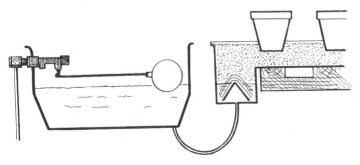

Cistern with Torbeck valve feeding water into pebble tray

- Use capillary matting on benches and extend it into a drainpipe laid horizontally to act as a reservoir.
- Use pebble trays to increase humidity.

The second and third options can be maintained automatically if they are connected to the mains and controlled by a cistern and Torbeck valve (see Two West's and Elliott catalogue).

Other options

Coldframes

People who do not have the space for, or need, a large greenhouse can overwinter tender plants and bring on others a bit earlier by other means.

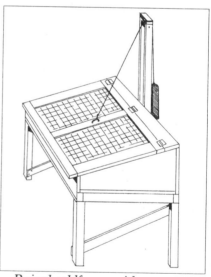

The traditional coldframe can be improved by raising its height and putting a counterbalance weight on the lid to make opening and closing easier. For safety reasons, plastic is preferable to glass and just as effective for a coldframe.

Raised coldframe with counter-weighted lid

Lean-to and mini-greenhouses

These purpose-built structures, which cost less and take up less space than the usual greenhouse, can be very effective if chosen carefully. Since access is the main problem, models with wider opening fronts or sides are the best. If you are consultaing a catalogue, such as Agriframes, look at it carefully and ask for all the dimensions before you order.

Some models, suitable for growing tomatoes in growbags, vary in quality from well-made cedar to aluminum frames with a plastic bag thrown over them. If you are using a growbag, then consider using growbag holders for stability or cane supports to which ties can be attached. A good alternative is the Hold-n-grow growbag planter which has holes for canes and can also be easily converted into a propagator.(Suppliers: Agriframes; Two West's and Elliott; Chichester Garden Products)

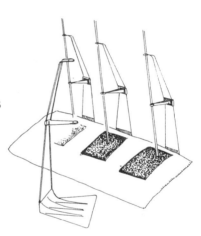

Growbag with wire cane support

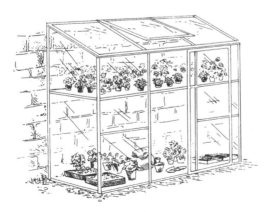

Lean-to greenhouse

STORAGE AND MAINTENANCE OF EQUIPMENT

When planning any storage area - whether a shed, locker or covered rack - access is the most important aspect to consider.

Some people take the easy option and leave some old tools scattered about the garden. This has obvious drawbacks but also some practical benefits if your garden is secure and/or your tools are of little financial importance to you. The plastic Fiskars handtools, for instance, can be left out safely, but remember that metal tools may go rusty and could be used by a burglar to break into your house!

Sheds

A specialist manufacturer of garden sheds is most likely to meet the needs of a wheelchair user and many such companies will usually be found locally. Once you have acquired a shed, provide plenty of storage space by putting in adjustable shelving, hooks and toolholders.

Toolholders

Whether you have a shed, locker or lean-to shelter, tools should be stored on some kind of rack. A jumble of tools in a corner will irritate both able-bodied and disabled gardeners alike.

Toolracks are available in many shapes and forms - from DIY versions using long nails

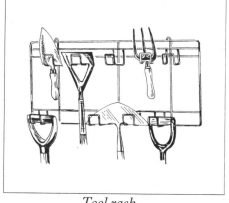

Tool rack

and screws to the purpose-built versions particular to each range of interchangeable tools, such as Gardena and Wolf. Whatever you do, have at least one toolrack or regret it for years to come! (Suppliers: Wolf-Tools; Gardena)

Tool locker

Cleaning your tools

A good tip is to tie an old scrubbing or washing-up brush near your hosepipe and get into the habit of washing the mud off the tools before putting them away.

Combined potting and tool shed laid out for wheelchair access

Oiling tools

Once the tools have been cleaned, they ought to be lubricated. This will not only extend their lifespan but ensure that they remain easy to use - an important factor for the disabled gardener. A well-tried method is to clean them with a rag impregnated with oil (3 in 1 for, instance). But a cleaner, more modern way is to use a can of Teflon spray and then wipe the tools lightly with a clean rag or kitchen towel.

Sharpening tools

A very simple and easy-to-use tool for sharpening knives, shears and pruners is the Diafold Diamond Whetstone which is a small strip of metal covered in a diamond abrasive. You simply fold the metal blade out, wet it and then rub the tool to be sharpened on the whetstone. Only one hand is needed if you use a vice and it produces no sparks or dangerous splinters.
(Suppliers: DMT Inc, via toolshops; DIY centres)

3 Tools and techniques for your particular situation

This chapter gives helpful tips on the type of equipment that is suitable for people with specific conditions and also guidance on how to use it.

The recommendations are based on work carried out at the Mary Marlborough specialist disability centre in Oxford which strives to help people to continue gardening despite their age or any disability they may have inherited or developed.

The people seen at the Centre range from those with minor conditions to those with very severe disabilities. With the aid of over 300 items of equipment, 25 years' experience, and advice from physiotherapists, occupational therapists and engineers, the Centre can usually offer a number of solutions to a wide range of problems.

To make this chapter easier to follow, it is divided into categories of conditions that need specific advice. It is therefore possible that people with complex problems will have to consult more than one section.

Wheelchair users and gardeners with visual impairments may need more advice than it is possible to include in the publication.

If you would like further information or advice, please write (enclosing a large stamped addressed envelope) to the Mary Marlborough Centre or to Horticultural Therapy giving specific details of your particular needs.

FOR PEOPLE WHO HAVE DIFFICULTY BENDING OR KNEELING

Most gardeners, at some time in their lives, find it difficult to bend or kneel. Luckily, therefore, this is one of the easiest problems to solve. While 'messing about' with our hands in the soil brings us closer to nature and can be a pleasureable process, it is rarely neccesary. With modern long-handled, well designed tools nearly every task can be completed standing up and with a straight back. If you have problems with your back or are unable to get down to ground level, you will need (and can) develop a technique to work completely upright. If you want to kneel but just need a bit of help, try using a kneeler stool.

Taking weeding as an example, the weeds can be picked up with a leaf grabber, scooped up with the underside of a lawn rake, or picked up with the Helping Hand. If that is too difficult, they can be raked into a heap and left to dry out.

Weeding the patio can be done with the patio knife or Weed Wand flame gun. Pruning can be dealt with by using long-handled pruners, such as the Darlac Snapper, or even with a saw fitted to a long handle.

Cutting the edge of the lawn can be made easier if you use lawnshears which are longer than the usual type. To achieve the same effect, you could fit some extension tubes to your existing shears.

Digging presents the biggest problem but this can be dealt with either by adopting a no-dig technique or using special tools. For conventional digging, especially in allotements, the Wolf Soil Miller is useful on lighter soil. The Garden Claw offers a new approach.

For people who have only a minor problem or prefer a conventional fork or spade, a number of solutions can be found.

- First, get a longer, ergonomically designed tool, or try a smaller toolhead on a long handle.
- Fit an auxiliary handle. Most importantly, try to think about your technique as you work and work slowly, remembering to take plenty of rests.

Loading things into a wheelbarrow can be easily accomplished with a special barrow that can be lowered so that you can push or drag things into it. A simple technique used by many professionals is to load materials into a large canvas tarpaulin and then drag it to the place where they are needed.

Tools for people who find it difficult to bend

Ascender lift wheelbarrow (see p 56);
Blackwall grabber rake (see p 61);
canvas tarpaulin (see above);
Darlac Snapper (see p 41);
Garden Claw (see p 40);
Helping Hand (see p 61);
lawn rake (or handrake) (see p 61);
leaf grabber (see p 61);
long-handled garden saw (see p 44);
long-handled lawn shears (see p 47);
long-handled trowels and hand forks (see pp 35- 36);
scuffle hoe (see p 31);
Spear and Jackson Backsaver Range forks and spades (see p 34);
Weed Wand (see p 31);
Wilkinson Sword Power Range forks and spades (see p 34);
Wilkinson Sword Swoe (see p 26);
Wolf Soil Miller (see p 39);
Wolf weed extractor (see p 28).

TOOLS FOR PEOPLE WHO FIND IT DIFFICULT TO BEND

Wilkinson Classic Swoe

Garden Claw

Wolf weed extractor

Extra-long-handled spade with auxiliary handle

Leaf grabber

Long-handled hand fork

FOR PEOPLE WHO HAVE A WEAK GRIP OR PAINFUL UPPER LIMBS

Many people suffer from conditions such as arthritis which can cause both pain and weakness in the hands and arms. People with these problems can find pruning and digging difficult. These tasks often entail using considerable force and pressure, although digging involves more movement.

Both activities can aggravate the pain so that the person's range of movement is impaired; they can even cause arthritic conditions to flare up. During such a flare up all gardening activities may have to be postponed. If you can prevent this happening it is therefore well worth the effort.

For people who find that they are no longer able to grip things firmly, lighter and easier-to-use tools are recommended.

For arthritis sufferers the same is true, except that they must be particularly careful to protect their knuckles, wrists and elbows from excess strain which can cause inflammation of the joints. Techniques involving special handles and arm supports made by the Centre's engineers have been used at the Mary Marlborough Centre for 25 years, and newly designed equipment is now available via mail order.

Gripping tools

Gripping tools with a shaft-type handle can cause excess strain on the small joints of the hand, and it is now widely acknowledged that a pistol-like grip is safer and it definately feels more comfortable. Tools with this type of grip are available or you can fit a grip to your own tools.

The pistol grip helps to protect the hand joints but leaves the wrist vulnerable. To overcome this, an arm support — like that fitted to a crutch — can be slotted into a bar that fits into the back of the pistol grip.

The hardness of the tools' handles can also adversely affect your hands. The cheapest solution is to fit Rubberzote padding onto the handles. This is a medical quality foam similar to the foam lagging fitted to copper pipes; alternatively, a number of tools with padded or moulded handles are available.

Tools for people with reduced grip

CK ratchet pruners (see p 42); Fiskars plastic fork and trowel (see p 36); Peta add-on handles (see p 38); Peta pistol-grip tools with arm supports (see pp 36 -37).

Plastic handled ratchet pruners

FOR PEOPLE WITH REDUCED STAMINA OR WHO SUFFER FROM CHRONIC FATIGUE

While everyone can identify with this problem at some stage in their lives, conditions such as angina or asthma can cause serious and chronic problems. Chronic pain also causes fatigue as can muscle weakness which may be associated with ageing or disability.

One obvious way to deal with fatigue is to delegate the most tiring tasks to someone else! However, assuming there are still things you are able, and want, to do in the garden, the key word to remember is 'pacing'.

First, for safety reasons, it is essential that you do not try to do too much. The best strategy is to rest before you get over tired and then return for another session.

Taking breaks

Most people can gauge their own abilities and take breaks at the right time. Some of us, however, get carried away and, if not reminded, will do too much. One helpful tip is to ask a partner or friend to stop you at intervals, or use a stopwatch or kitchen timer and organise your tasks in blocks with breaks in between, eg mow the lawn, have a ten minute break; prune the shrubs, have a ten minute break; water the tubs, have a

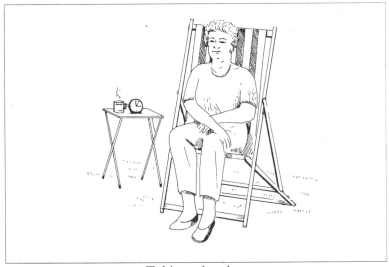

Taking a break

ten minute break. Leaving chairs and reading materials nearby may also help to remind you.

'Pacing' allied with the use of lightweight tools can reduce fatigue and increase efficiency. The Swoe is an efficent weeding tool as it is light and cuts backwards, forwards and sideways. Smaller forks, spades, rakes, brooms and other tools are available.

Being well organised

Being well organised and taking all the tools you need for a job is also important. Toolbelts and aprons or even big pockets are very useful and a caddy with a rubbish bag holder for larger tools will save you from having to make numerous trips back to the shed. Likewise, making sure that multiple compost heaps and waterbutts are strategically placed could save valuable energy.

Power tools, like hedge trimmers and strimmers, may be appropriate for some people. Cordless tools, like the Black and Decker range, are ideal for small jobs and the battery duration can help you to pace yourself. A number of self-propelled lawn mowers are available and the Qualcast QX system also enables you to use your mower for raking and scarifying.

Wilkinson Sword Swoe

Tools to help reduce fatigue

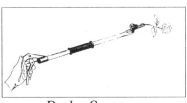

Darlac Snapper

Darlac Snapper (see p 41); cordless hedge trimmer (see p 48); cordless strimmer (see p 69);

Garden Claw (see p 40);
long-handled pruner (see p 43);
Qualcast QX system (see p 66);
Victory deck broom (see p 61);
Weed Wand (see p 32);
Wilkinson Sword Swoe (see p 26).

FOR PEOPLE WHO WORK WITH ONE HAND/ARM

While most tasks can be undertaken with one hand,
some, such as digging, seem impossible at first. In fact,
digging safely in the conventional way with a full-size
tool is virtually impossible. However, a long-handled
hand fork with an arm support can be used for smaller
areas.

Another approach is to ask yourself if digging is
really neccesary. The no-dig technique has been
successful at Ryton Organic Gardens near Coventry for
many years. By dividing digging areas into strips and not
walking over them, the soil does not become compacted
and needs less cultivation.

The Wolf Soil Miller can be
used with one arm and, as is
the case with any long-
handled tool, a pistol grip
and arm support will
increase power and control
and reduce strain.

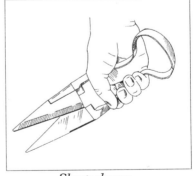

Sheep shears

Wheelbarrows can also
cause problems, but some
models with two wheels and
pram-type handles can be used.

Tools such as shears have to be operated with two
hands but can be replaced with electric hedge
trimmersand or single-handed shears for softer foliage.

Large branch pruners can be replaced by a saw and even extended on a long handle.

Tools for use with one hand/arm

Trailer Barrow

Darlac Snapper (see p 41);
Garden Twin Barrow (see p 56);
lightweight hedge trimmers (see p 48);
Peta add-on handles with arm support cuff (see pp 36 - 38):
sheep shears (see p 46):
One-handed shears (see p 46);
Trailer Barrow (see p 55);
Wilkinson Sword long-handled hand fork (see p 35):
Wolf Cut and Grip secateurs (see p 42);
Wolf Soil Miller (with Peta add-on handle and arm support cuff (see p 38).

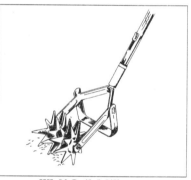
Wolf Soil Miller

FOR PEOPLE GARDENING FROM A WHEELCHAIR

For anyone gardening from a wheelchair, the important factors to bear in mind are the weight and length of the tools and finding the best way to move equipment and materials. If the user has two strong arms, he or she should have few problems working with plants at ground level if the correct tools are used. The Wilkinson Sword Swoe and the Darlac Snapper long-handled pruner are ideal, as is the Baronet Weedpuller which can be used for weeding to make small holes for planting and act as a tool to place the plant in the hole.

Handling materials

The main problem for wheelchair users is not so much the tools themselves but handling materials.

One-handed wheelbarrows and garden trucks are not very practical on anything but the smoothest surfaces like patios. For many people the answer may be to have a laptray with a box on it. A beanbag laptray with a large tupperware container or seedtray attached to it with Velcro is a good idea.

Tools should, if possible, be carried one at a time or on the fold-down caddies that attach to the front tubes of the wheelchair. These lightweight plastic caddies are very strong and can be adjusted to carry bags and boxes as large as a big suitcase. Tools with interchangeable heads are useful since only one handle needs to be carried into the garden.

The various toolheads could be carried out to the garden together or kept outside in a locker or weatherproof container.

Organising tools

It is important to organise not only the carrying equipment but also the tools and materials so that they are easily accessible. Toolracks, open shelving, baskets on wheels and an accessible bench are essential. A plastic or wooden, low-fronted tidy tray on the bench will help to prevent compost from piling up on your lap when potting up.

Gardening from an electric wheelchair has some advantages but presents other problems. The increased mobility is useful but the sides of the chair and joystick controls often restrict movement. Electric wheelchair users are also likely to have weaker arms and will therefore have a more restricted choice of tools.

Darlac Snapper

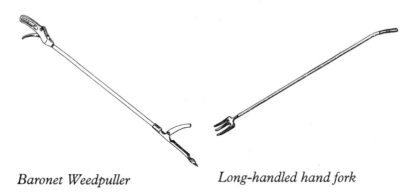

Baronet Weedpuller   *Long-handled hand fork*

While special equipment is essential for wheelchair users, garden design is equally important — more so than for any other group of gardeners with disabilities.

Tools for gardening from a wheelchair

Baronet Weedpuller (see p 27);
Darlac Snapper (see p 41);

interchangeable tools (Gardena; Wolf) (see pp 30, 31, 43, 44);
beanbag laptray (see p 91);
long-handled hand fork (see p 35);
raised hosepipe with watering stations and spray gun (Hozelock or Gardena) (see p 52);
Wilkinson Sword Swoe (see 26);
telescopic patio weeding knife (see p 29);
telescopic watering lance (see p 53).

FOR PEOPLE WITH A VISUAL IMPAIRMENT

The range of conditions and problems associated with having a visual impairment are extensive and complicated. The solutions usually involve developing techniques to suit each individual and constructing special equipment for measuring and guidance. While only a few ideas are discussed here, other sources of information cover the subject extensively and with great expertise.

The charity Horticultural Therapy produces a quarterly newsletter on tape and in Braille entitled *Come gardening*. Training weekends are also held, usually at horticutural colleges, at which visually impaired gardeners and experts in the field study the latest techniques. These weekends are so successful that many gardeners return each year to share ideas and experiences with people in similar situations.

Free of hazards

When considering design, a number of things ought to be taken into account. The layout of the garden should ensure that it it free of unnecessary hazards and make it possible for the gardener to have easy access to plants, equipment and materials.

The use of sounds from water features and windchimes may help people with a visual impairment to orientate themselves in the garden. Measured use of scented plants at key locations close to paths can provide position markers for totally blind gardeners, as can the use of different texture for paths and surfacing.

For partially sighted gardeners, non-reflective and contrasting coloured surfaces should be used rather than monotone or reflective surfaces like concrete. Bold and contrasting coloured plants when are also helpful for partially sighted people.

Importance of safety

Safety is especially important and care should be taken to keep soft fruit away from pathways, and thornless roses can be planted instead of the thorned variety. Handrails and tapping rails are other commonly used features. Cane toppers are even more essential for visually impaired garderners to protect the eyes and face from injury, although other types of plant support, such as Lynk stakes or support rings, may be more suitable than canes.

Tools with easy-to-find safety catches are available as are brightly coloured tools and other equipment. Yellow

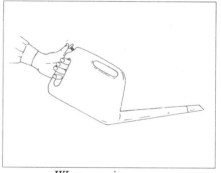

Watermatic can

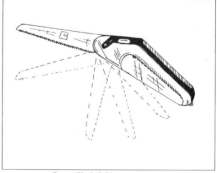

Small folding saw

rather than green hosepipe (supplied by Hozelock) could be used; if it is raised off the ground on hooks it will be easy to access and people will not trip over it.

When watering, the Watermatic can has a release mechanism so that users can gauge easily the amount of water released. Lastly, if falling over is a conern then safety glass or even plastic panels can be used in greenhouses and cold frames.

Tools for visually impaired gardeners

Toolbelts and aprons (see p 59);
folding saw (see p 45);
home-made measuring equipment (as advised by Horticultural Therapy and the RNIB);
Watermatic watering can (see p 50);
yellow hosepipe (see p 94).

FOR CHILDREN WITH DISABILITIES

As an activity for children, gardening has many benefits. It can be fun, creative and educational and is not expensive. Children also enjoy the fact that getting dirty while gardening is acceptable and appropriate and, because they usually start gardening on a small scale, the restrictions associated with having a disability are minimised.

The challenge, as always with children, is to stimulate and maintain their interest. This is easily done by using brightly coloured and dynamic plants that change quickly. Sunflowers, tomatoes, strawberries. Pumpkins, and flowering bulbs are ideal. Being able to eat the plant (safely) or give it away as a present is an added bonus that appeals to every gardener.

Scented plants can also be an attraction but remember that some children do not appear to like the powerful smell of many herbs. Care must be taken to avoid dangerous plants that may be toxic when eaten or cause skin reactions. (A full list is available from the Royal Horticultural Society.) Thorns can also be a hazard, but this can be avoided if thornless varieties of fruit and roses are chosen.

The type of gardening you choose to do with your child will depend on his or her age and mobility and on your own experience.

If the child is very small and may work on the ground, either sitting or lying down, take care to remove hard or sharp objects from the soil. A small child will find a light, open soil the easiest to handle. A coir-based compost is relatively clean to work with as well as being environmentally friendly.

Association with play

If possible, try to give each child his or her own particular patch of garden. This can be made even more attractive if ornaments and toys to reinforce the association with play are included. In addition, a sense of mystery, which appeals to most children, can be achieved by having lots of paths going in different directions and creating many secret and sheltered spaces.

For safety and educational reasons children should be encouraged to garden organically, ie without using chemicals, fertilisers or pesticides. Teaching children to pick up and remove snails, to encourage and collect. ladybirds and to befriend birds and frogs can teach them the elements of ecology as well as organic gardening.

Purpose-built tools

Very small children will probably be able to garden with household forks and serving spoons, while plastic cups can be used for watering. As they get older and more able, purpose-built tools are available. The Parasene range of 'little ones' is excellent but will probably need additional handles and further modification if used by a disabled child.

Supervising children while they are gardening is very important, especially if they are using tools (plastic tools are preferable to metal if possible). For further advice on adapting equipment for children, contact the Mary Marlborough Centre.

Tools for children

Beanbag laptrays (see p 91);
Fiskars plastic fork and trowel (see p 36);
old spoons and blunt forks;
Parasene 'little ones' (see p 96);
Peta add-on handles with arm support and Velcro cuff (see pp 36 - 38);
plastic forks and trowels;
Wolf D-grip handle (see p 38).

Appendix 1:

Agralan Ltd, The Old Brickyard, Ashton Keynes, Swindon, Wilts SN6 6QR (tel: 01285 860015; fax: 01285 860056)

— *Agriframes Ltd,* Charlwoods Road, East Grinstead, West Sussex RH19 2HG (tel: 01342 319111; fax: 01342 327233)

Allen Power Equipment, The Broadway, Didcot, Oxon OX11 8ES (tel: 01235 81393; fax: 01235 811491)

Alton Greenhouses Ltd, Station Works, Fenny Compton, Nr Leamington Spa, Warks CV33 0XB (tel: 01295 770795; fax: 01295 770748)

A Wright & Son Ltd, 16/18 Sidney Street, Sheffield S1 4RH (tel: 0114 2722677; fax: 0114 2787157)

— *Black and Decker Ltd,* Westpoint, The Grove, Slough, Berks SL1 1QQ (tel: 01753 511234; fax: 01753 551155)

Blackwall Products, 10 Glover Way, Parkside, Leeds, LS11 5JP (tel: 01132 761646; fax: 01132 713083)

Burgeon and Ball Ltd, La Plata Works, Holme Lane, Sheffield S6 4JY (tel: 0114 2338262; fax: 0114 2852518)

— *Ceka Garden Tools*, Ceka Works, Caernarvon Road, Pwllheli, Gwynedd LL53 5LH (tel:01758 701070; fax: 01758 701090)

Chichester Garden Products, Quarry Lane Industrial Estate, Chichester, West Sussex PO19 2NY (tel: 01243 779598) (products distributed by *David Miller*, 10 Park Road, Tunbridge Wells, Kent TN4 9JN (tel and fax: 01892 525733)

CLM Fabrications, Newtown, Offenham, Evesham, Worcs WR11 5RZ (tel: 01386 49094; fax: 01386 421605)

Corrie (JB) & Co Ltd, Petersfield, Hants GU32 3AP (tel: 01730 262552; fax: 01730 264915)

Croydex Co Ltd, Central Way Andover, Hants SP10 5AW (tel: 01264 358882; fax: 01264 336865)

— *Damar International Ltd*, 45 Humberstone Drive, Leicester, LE5 0RE (tel: 01533 764144; fax 01533 460663)

Darlac Products, 34 Slough Road, Datchet, Berkshire SL3 9AW (tel: 01753 547790; fax: 01753 580542)

— *Dan Medica Ltd*, 17 Crosslands Road, Worsley, Manchester M28 1JH (tel and fax: 0161 7020238)

Erin-Gardena (UK) Ltd, Dunhams Lane, Letchworth Garden City, Hertfordshire SG6 1BD (tel: 01462 475000; fax: 01462 482456)

— **Fiskars Ltd,** Brocastle Avenue, Waterton Industrial Estate, Bridgend, Mid Glamorgan CF1 3YN (tel: 01656 655595; fax: 01656 659582)

— **Flymo Ltd, Preston Road,** Aycliffe Industrial Estate, Newton Aycliffe, Co Durham DL5 6UP (tel: 01325 300303; fax: 01325 310339)

Gardena - see **Erin-Gardena (UK) Ltd**

GBL Wheelchairs Ltd, Units 3 & 4 Shield Drive, Brentford, Middlesex (tel: 0181 569 8955; fax: 0181 5605380)

Geeco Ltd, Gore Road Industrial Estate, New Milton, Hampshire BH25 6SE (tel: 01425 614600; fax: 01425 619463)

Glowcroft, Unit K2, Innsworth Technology Park, Innsworth Lane, Gloucester GL3 1DL (tel: 01452 731300; fax: 01452 731301)

Haemelin Ltd, The Washington Centre, Halesown Road, Netherton, West Midlands (tel: 01384 243243; fax: 01384 243242)

Harcoaster Ltd, Homes and Gardens Division, Windover Road, Huntingdon, Cambs PE13 7EE (tel: 01480 52323; fax: 01480 413203)

Helping Hand Company, Unit 9L, Bromyard Trading Estate, Ledbury HR8 1NS (tel: 01531 635678; fax: 01531 635670)

Hozelock Ltd, Haddenham, Aylesbury, Bucks HP17 8JD (tel: 01844 291881; fax: 01844 290344)

Jemp Engineering Ltd, Canal Estate, Station Road, Langley, Berks Sl3 6EG (tel: 01753 548327; fax: 01753 580137)

Joseph Enterprises UK, Suite 5, 2nd Floor, Octagon Court, High Wycombe, Bucks HP11 2HS (tel: 01494 464653; fax: 01494 464554)

Ivyline, 13-15 Bedford Street, Coventry, CV1 3EW (tel: 01203 630433 (no fax))

MCI Timply Ltd, 6 Culver Court, Malting Lane, Much Hadham, Herts SG10 6AN (tel: 01279 842288; fax: 01279 842299)

Miracle Garden Care Ltd, Salisbury House, Wayside Park, Cattershall Lane, Godalming, Surrey GU7 1XE (tel: 01483 410210; fax: 01483 410220)

Newbrook Products Ltd, Swaffham Bulbeck, Cambs CB5 0LU (tel: 01223 812729; fax: 01223 813199)

New Waves Marketing, Lilac Cottage, King's Lane, Flore, Northants NN6 4LQ (tel: 01327 341366; fax: 01327 341219)

Parasene - see ***New Waves Marketing***

Par-Fox Products, High Street, Golborne,
Warrington, Cheshire WA33 3AN (tel: 01942 726862;
fax: 01942 722080)

Parklines (Buildings) Ltd, Park House, 501 Green
Lanes, Palmers Green, London N13 4BS (tel: 0181 886
0011; fax: 0121 446 5991)

⤚ ***Peta (UK) Ltd,*** Marks Hall, Margaret Roding,
Dunmow, Essex CM6 1QT (tel and fax: 01245
231811)

Plantpak Ltd, Burnham Road, Mundon, Maldon,
Essex CP9 6NT (tel: 01621 740140; fax 01621
742400)

Plysu Housewares Ltd, Wolseley Road, Kempston,
Bedford MK42 7UD (tel: 01234 841771; fax: 01234
841037)

Qualcast-Atco Ltd, Suffolk Works, Stowmarket,
Suffolk IP14 1EU (tel: 01449 742000; fax: 01449
675444)

Redashe Ltd, Unit 11, Hewitts Industrial Estate,
Elmbridge Road, Cranleigh, Surrey GU6 8LW (tel:
01483 275774; fax: 01483 277947)

Robinsons Greenhouses Ltd, Robinsons House, First
Avenue, Millbrook, Southampton SO15 0LG (tel:
01703 703355; fax: 01703 705588)

Spear and Jackson - see *Dan Medica Ltd*

Standard Manufacturing Co, 55 Woods Lane, Derby DE3 3UD (tel: 01332 343369; fax: 01332 381531)

Trailer Barrow Company, Buxted, East Sussex TN22 4LW (tel: 01825 748200; fax: 01825 761212)

Two West's and Elliott Catologue, Unit 4, Carrwood Road, Sheepbridge Industrial Estate, Chesterfield, Derbyshire S41 9RH (tel: 01246 451077; fax: 01246 260115)

Wilkinson Sword - see *Fiskars*

Wolf-Tools Ltd, Ross-on-Wye, Herefordshire HP9 5NE (tel: 01989 767600; fax: 01989 765589)

Appendix 2:

USEFUL ORGANISATIONS

Disabled Living Centres Council, 1st Floor, Winchester House, 11 Cranmer Road, London SW9 6EJ (tel: 0171 820 0567; fax: 0171 735 0278) (a number of centres stock tools and equipment)

Gardening for Disabled Trust, Frettendon House, Frettendon, Kent TN17 2DG *or* Woodgate House, Beckley, Rye, East Sussex TN31 6UH (*written enquiries only*)

Horticultural Therapy, Goulds Ground, Vallis Way, Frome, Somerset BA11 3DW (tel and fax: 01373 464782) (offers a range of services to individuals and projects and publishes numerous leaflets and books)

Mary Marlborough Centre, Windmill Lane, Headington, Oxford OX3 7LD (fax: 01865 227463) (*written enquiries only*)

REMAP , Hazeldene, Ightham, Sevenoaks, Kent, TN15 9AD (tel: 01732 883818; fax 01732 886238)

Ryton Organic Gardens, Henry Doubleday Research Association, Ryton-on-Dunsmore, Coventry CV8 3LG (*written enquiries only*)

Royal Horticultural Society, 80 Vincent Square, London SW1 2PB (tel: 0171 834 4333; fax: 0171 630 6060)

Royal National Institute for the Blind (RNIB), 224 Great Portland Street, London W1N 6AA (tel: 0171 388 1266; fax: 0171 388 2034)

Appendix 3:

FURTHER READING

Brickell, C (ed). *Royal Horticultural Society's Encyclopaedia of gardening.* Dorling Kindersley, 1992

Hessayon, Dr DG. *Container expert; Easy care gardening expert; Greenhouse expert; Tree and shrub expert.* PBI Publications

Horticultural Therapy, *Come gardening* (quarterly magazine, Braille and on tape only). HT

Reader's Digest. *The gardening year.* RD, 1982 (4th ed)

Spurgeon, T. *Getting on with gardening.* (large print, Braille and on tape) RNIB, Peterborough, 1997

Stoneham, T and Thoday, P. *Landscape design for elderly and disabled people.* Packard Publishing, 1994

Wiles, R. *Garden structures, RHS's Encyclopaedia of practical gardening.* Mitchell Beazley Publishers, 1992

Index